D1034107

A VISUAL HISTORY OF THE WORLD

A VISUAL HISTORY OF SHIPS AND NAVIGATION

TITANIC

ROSEN
PUBLISHING

ALBERTO MORENO
DE LA FUENTE

This edition published in 2017 by
The Rosen Publishing Group, Inc.
29 East 21st Street
New York, NY 10010

Library of Congress Cataloging-in-Publication Data

Names: Moreno de la Fuente, Alberto.
Title: A visual history of ships and navigation / Alberto Moreno de la Fuente.
Description: New York : Rosen Publishing, 2017. | Series: A visual history of the world | Includes bibliographical references and index..
Identifiers: ISBN 9781499465945 (library bound)
Subjects: LCSH: Ships—History—Juvenile literature. | Navigation—History—Juvenile literature.
Classification: LCC VM150.D45 2017| DDC 623.82009—dc23

Manufactured in Malaysia

Metric Conversion Chart

1 inch = 2.54 centimeters; 25.4 millimeters	1 cup = 250 milliliters
1 foot = 30.48 centimeters	1 ounce = 28 grams
1 yard = .914 meters	1 fluid ounce = 30 milliliters
1 square foot = .093 square meters	1 teaspoon = 5 milliliters
1 square mile = 2.59 square kilometers	1 tablespoon = 15 milliliters
1 ton = .907 metric tons	1 quart = .946 liters
1 pound = 454 grams	355 degrees F = 180 degrees Celsius
1 mile = 1.609 kilometers	

©2016 Editorial Sol90
Barcelona – Buenos Aires
All Rights Reserved
Editorial Sol90, S.L

Original Idea Nuria Cicero
Editorial Coordination Alberto Hernández
Editorial Team Alberto Moreno de la Fuente, Luciana Rosende, Virginia Iris Fernández, Pablo Pineau, Matías Loewy, Joan Soriano, Mar Valls, Leandro Jema
Proofreaders Marta Kordon, Edgardo D'Elio
Design María Eugenia Hiriart
Layout Laura Ocampo, Clara Miralles, Paola Fornasaro

Photography Age Fotostock, Getty Images, Science Photo Library, National Geographic, Latinstock, Album, ACI, Cordon Press
Illustrations and Infographics Trexel Animation, Trebol Animation, WOW Studio, Sebastián Giacobino, Néstor Taylor, Nuts Studio, Steady in Lab, 3DN, Federico Combi, Pablo Aschei, Leonardo César, 4D News, Rise Studio, Ariel Roldán, Dorian Vandegrift, Zoom Desarrollo Digitales, Marcelo Regalado.

Contents

Introduction

The history of **navigation** is the history of the human desire to conquer the sea and explore beyond the horizon. Since ancient times, coastal towns or those living along rivers and lakes built vessels to fish or move in the water. From that to going out to explore and conquer other territories there is only one step.

The old ships were powered by **oars** and **sails**. For centuries these were the means of propulsion of ships which became more efficient, powerful and larger. In the Middle Ages, Arab, Viking, Byzantine and Chinese peoples and European kingdoms had a key point for their expansion and power in naval fleets and maritime trade. In the fifteenth and sixteenth centuries, at the beginning of the Modern Age, ships capable of making long ocean journeys, carracks and caravels appeared; they were protagonists of the discovery of a new continent, America, and of the exploration of the world beyond the horizon. New transoceanic trade routes were opened, while warships starred the greatest naval battles in history.

The invention of the **steam** engine in the late eighteenth century started a new era in the history of navigation. Throughout the nineteenth century, there appeared liners capable of carrying thousands of passengers, river vessels performing regular services and the first battleships propelled by this system. In the twentieth century, the internal combustion **engine** was invented, which definitely displaced steam propulsion, and towards the end of the century, the first **nuclear**-powered ships and submarines were built.

At present, although as regards transatlantic services the ship seems to have been defeated by aircraft for decades, it continues to play a hugely important role in the transportation of persons, though for smaller distances. Thousands of ferries, passenger boats and ships of various drafts constantly navigate rivers and seas, notwithstanding that **world trade** has moved, for centuries, by water, and now it stars huge container ships, while submarines and aircraft carriers are essential parts of the largest and most modern armies in the world.

Chronology

8th century BC

▶ GREEK TRIREME
The Greek naval hegemony for over four centuries was based on its powerful ships with three rows of oars.

Third century BC

▶ ROMAN SHIP
The Roman Empire turned the galley into the type of fundamental vessel for its powerful fleet.

15th century

▶ CARAVELS AND CARRACKS
Prepared for long journeys, these ships were used by explorers to reach the "New World."

▶ TREASURE SHIP
This is the name given to the giant ships used by the Chinese Admiral Zheng He in his seven expeditions to Asia and Africa.

3000 BC

▶ EGYPTIANS
They are the first navigators of which there are records. The importance of the Nile caused them to develop different types of boats.

1200 BC

▶ PHOENICIANS
Great traders and sailors, they dominated the Mediterranean with their Gaulos and bireme ships.

8th to 9th century

▶ VIKINGS
Aboard their famous drekar, they spread terror in all the coasts of northern Europe and they even reached the Mediterranean.

1807

▶ STEAMBOAT
The *Clermont* was the first steamboat that worked successfully. In 1919, another steam vessel, the *Savannah*, successfully crossed the Atlantic.

1820

▶ THE *HMS BEAGLE*
Charles Darwin made this brig transformed into a barque famous, with which he conducted three scientific expeditions around the world.

1912

▶ *TITANIC*
The sinking of the legendary British liner, the biggest ship built so far, shocked the world. There were 1,514 victims.

1918

▶ AIRCRAFT CARRIER
That year, the first aircraft carrier began to be designed for such purpose: the *HMS Hermes*. Said ships would be key in World War II.

16th to 17th century

▶ GALLEYS AND GALLEONS
Mostly used ships for both military and trade purposes by the great imperial powers during the Modern Age.

▶ TURTLE SHIPS
Also called *Geobukseon*, the warships of the Korean Admiral Yi Sun-sin are characterized for having an armor-like shell similar to that of a turtle.

1858

▶ BATTLESHIP
France built the first warship with a hull completely shielded with iron, the *Gloire*. This marked the beginning of the battleships era.

1906

▶ DREADNOUGHT
It was a type battleship that dominated the twentieth century. They were powered by steam turbines and their heavy armament had a unique caliber.

1955

▶ NUCLEAR PROPULSION
The US submarine *Nautilus*, which crossed the North Pole under the polar ice cap, was the pioneer in the field of nuclear marine propulsion.

20th to 21st century

▶ CRUISES
Since the second half of the twentieth century, there has been a proliferation of large and luxurious ocean liners, such as the *Queen Mary* or *Queen Elizabeth*, destined to leisure travel.

Early navigators

Chapter 1

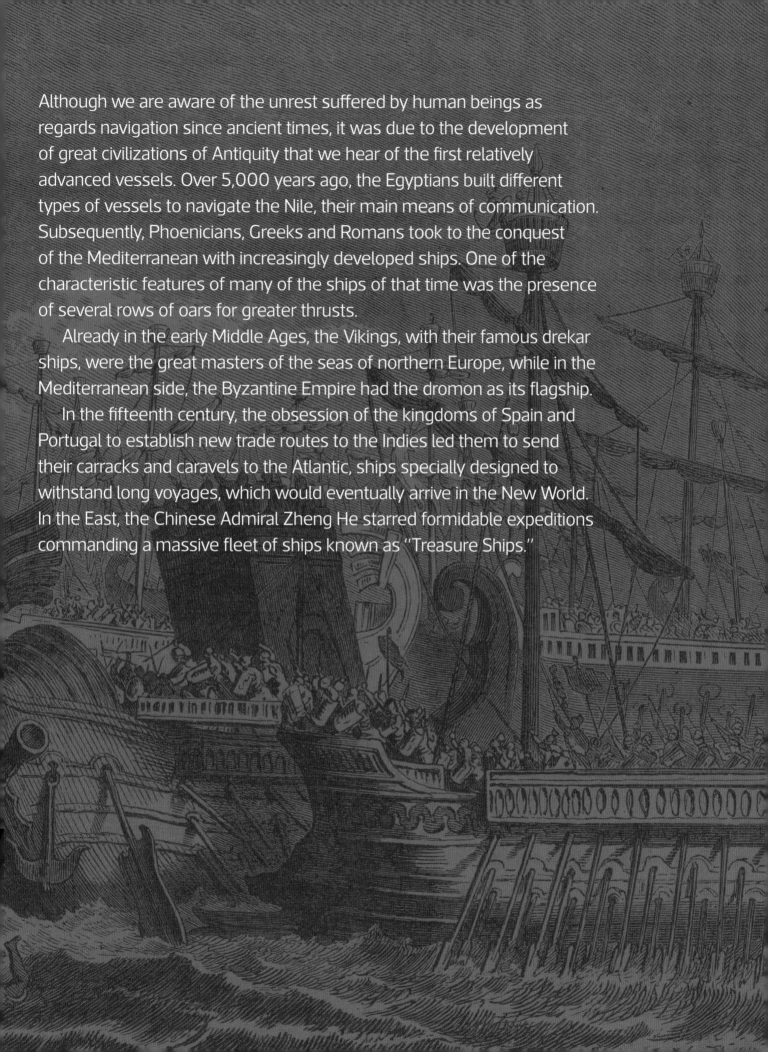

Although we are aware of the unrest suffered by human beings as regards navigation since ancient times, it was due to the development of great civilizations of Antiquity that we hear of the first relatively advanced vessels. Over 5,000 years ago, the Egyptians built different types of vessels to navigate the Nile, their main means of communication. Subsequently, Phoenicians, Greeks and Romans took to the conquest of the Mediterranean with increasingly developed ships. One of the characteristic features of many of the ships of that time was the presence of several rows of oars for greater thrusts.

Already in the early Middle Ages, the Vikings, with their famous drekar ships, were the great masters of the seas of northern Europe, while in the Mediterranean side, the Byzantine Empire had the dromon as its flagship.

In the fifteenth century, the obsession of the kingdoms of Spain and Portugal to establish new trade routes to the Indies led them to send their carracks and caravels to the Atlantic, ships specially designed to withstand long voyages, which would eventually arrive in the New World. In the East, the Chinese Admiral Zheng He starred formidable expeditions commanding a massive fleet of ships known as "Treasure Ships."

The sea and navigation

We will never know who had the idea, many years ago, of constructing a boat and jump into the sea. In any case, this procedure evolved to become the main mode of transport for long distances until the arrival of the aircraft.

The lure of the unknown

From the earliest times, mankind has felt the vital need to venture into the sea, either for food or to explore new horizons. Probably, at first they used logs, and then rafts made of logs tied together with vines, then canoes, kayaks and increasingly sophisticated boats driven by oars first and sails later. These were the first steps of navigation, the oldest way to transport people massively in the history of humankind.

MASTS
Their mission is to hold sails and withstand the force of the wind that sails convey. The yards are sticks crossed to hold several sails.

How to move boats

Achieving an efficient thrust on the surface of the water was a constant concern for sailors. Here, we review the main methods.

Oar
The most primitive form to thrust boats forward. The number of oars increased at the same time the size of the boats varied.

Sail
Another early form of propel boats, was to take advantage of the wind. Modern sails helped propelling against the wind direction.

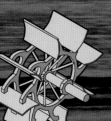

Paddle-wheel
The first powerboats used steam power to move a paddle wheel.

Helix propellers
They turn when completely submerged and they are much more efficient than the paddle-wheels.

HULL
The frame of the ships was originally made of light and less permeable timber, but in the nineteenth century iron was introduced followed by steel.

Why they float

Being hollow inside, the hull of the vessels is less dense than water, even in the case of great ocean liners. This, jointly with the vertical force exerted by the water in accordance with the Archimedes Principle is what makes boats stay afloat.

PIONEERS
Although Egyptians are the first navigators of which there are records, it is believed that various indigenous peoples had built primitive canoes about 8,000 years ago.

Sailing

Very early in its history, Mankind used wind power to propel their boats so they could travel long distances in the sea. This was essential for trade and wars of conquest since they were able to transport large quantities of goods or troops with a lesser consumption of energy. With the application of steam and, subsequently, the internal combustion engines, sailing vessels were relegated to sport and recreational activity.

Types of sails

Sailors refined the sails to better harness the power of wind, to navigate in calm weather or even against the wind.

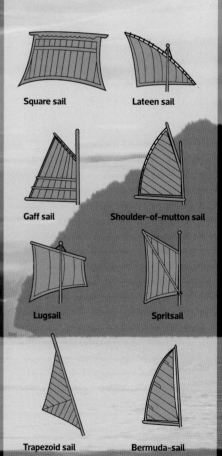

Square sail

Lateen sail

Gaff sail

Shoulder-of-mutton sail

Lugsail

Spritsail

Trapezoid sail

Bermuda-sail

HOW THEY NAVIGATE
Sailboats receive different forces, especially from the wind. And the combination of sails and rudder can generate a resultant force with a specific direction towards which the boat will sail.

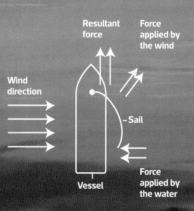

Resultant force

Force applied by the wind

Wind direction

Sail

Vessel

Force applied by the water

The "wheel" of vessels

The rudder is almost as old as the ships. It is known that the Egyptians used a large paddle to guide their ships from one side of the stern, the so-called oar rudder. In the thirteenth century, it was replaced by the stern-post rudder, perpendicular to the keel attached to a rotating wheel on the deck.

Deflector rudder. Its movement affects water flow and causes the change of direction of the vessels.

Egyptian vessels

Given the vital importance of the Nile River (main means of communication), the Egyptians have developed, since ancient times, different types of vessels such as boats made of papyrus, passenger and funerary ships and warships.

Sailing the Nile

The classic Egyptian ships had an elevated bow and stern, and also a mast and a square sail resting on the lower yard; the upper one was mobile. When sailing the Nile towards the north and cocurrently, they used the oars, and when they were directed towards the south, the sail was unfolded to seize the favorable wind. In the Mediterranean, similar double-rudder ships (the kebenit) were used, made from wood, and performing coastal navigation.

FORECASTLE
It had two castles, one on the aft and one in the bow, where most soldiers gathered, generally archers aiming at enemy ships.

Subsequent ships

Throughout the centuries, the Egyptians copied the models of vessels belonging to other peoples such as Greeks, Phoenicians and Romans. For example, the quinquereme and trihemiolia.

35 m
Trihemiolia (III Century BC)

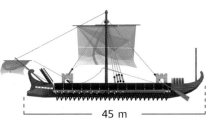
45 m
Quinquereme (IV century BC to I Century)

TECHNICAL SHEET

▸ **Type:** Monoreme galley
▸ **Crew:** Unknown.
▸ **Dimensions:**

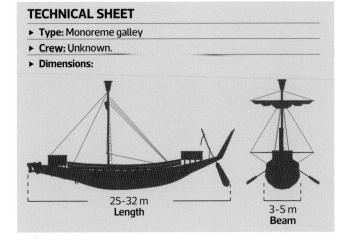

25-32 m
Length

3-5 m
Beam

BOW RAM
Made of wood reinforced with bronze, usually representing the head of a lion.

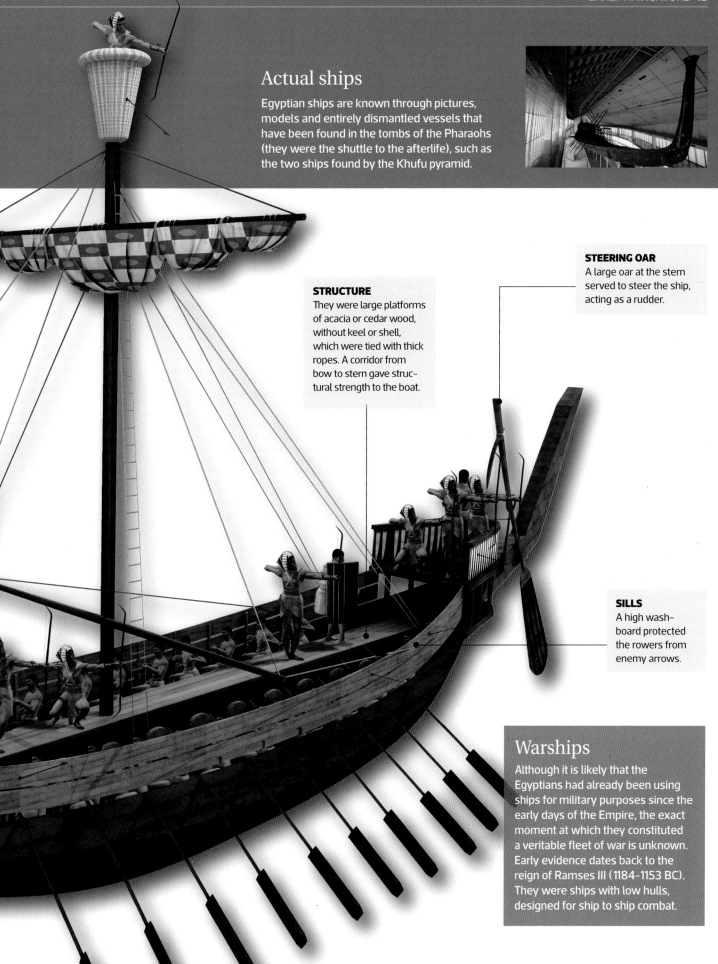

Actual ships

Egyptian ships are known through pictures, models and entirely dismantled vessels that have been found in the tombs of the Pharaohs (they were the shuttle to the afterlife), such as the two ships found by the Khufu pyramid.

STRUCTURE
They were large platforms of acacia or cedar wood, without keel or shell, which were tied with thick ropes. A corridor from bow to stern gave structural strength to the boat.

STEERING OAR
A large oar at the stern served to steer the ship, acting as a rudder.

SILLS
A high washboard protected the rowers from enemy arrows.

Warships

Although it is likely that the Egyptians had already been using ships for military purposes since the early days of the Empire, the exact moment at which they constituted a veritable fleet of war is unknown. Early evidence dates back to the reign of Ramses III (1184-1153 BC). They were ships with low hulls, designed for ship to ship combat.

The Phoenician vessel

The Phoenicians were the major promoters of market exchanges in the Mediterranean during the first millennium BC. They owned the riches enclaves as regards metals thanks to their innovative ships (for commercial and battle purposes), their seamanship and courage.

Owners of the Mediterranean

Being expert navigators, the main trade route of the Phoenicians ran from the city of Tyre (now in south Lebanon) to their factories in Gadir (now Cadiz in southern Spain). In total, they sailed 4,600 kilometers in 50 days, stopping at various ports, with ships from 20 to 30 meters in length carrying a hundred tons of merchandise. During the trips they used to colonize other peoples and they even managed to circumnavigate Africa.

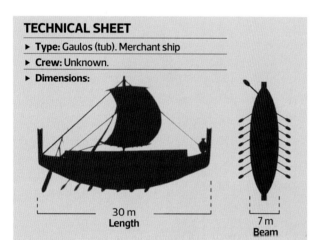

TECHNICAL SHEET

▸ **Type:** Gaulos (tub). Merchant ship
▸ **Crew:** Unknown.
▸ **Dimensions:**

30 m
Length

7 m
Beam

The oldest ones

In 1988, the remains of two Phoenician ships were found in Mazarrón (Spain). Carbon 14 revealed that the ships dated from the years 650-600 BC; therefore, they are the oldest vessels ever found except for the ritual boat of Khufu.

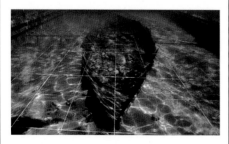

Mazarrón 2. One of the Phoenician ships is protected at 20 m from the coast and 5 m deep.

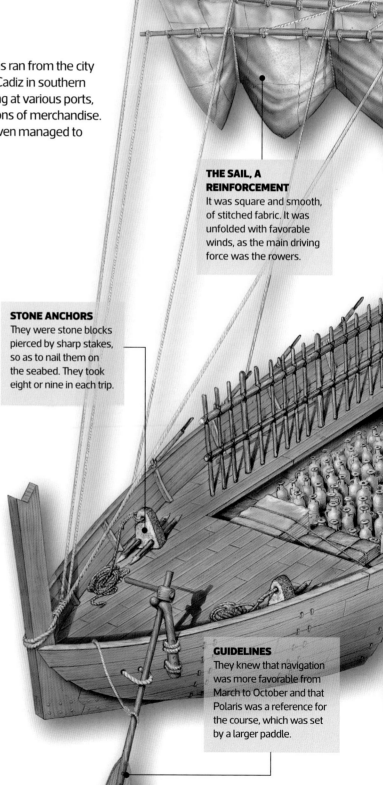

THE SAIL, A REINFORCEMENT
It was square and smooth, of stitched fabric. It was unfolded with favorable winds, as the main driving force was the rowers.

STONE ANCHORS
They were stone blocks pierced by sharp stakes, so as to nail them on the seabed. They took eight or nine in each trip.

GUIDELINES
They knew that navigation was more favorable from March to October and that Polaris was a reference for the course, which was set by a larger paddle.

The most lucrative goods

Some of the best goods of the Phoenicians were the purple fabrics dyed with murex segregation (a common mollusk from the Phoenicia coastline), the valuable cedar wood (ideal for building boats and houses due to its resistance to water) and jewels and other objects made of gold, silver, ivory and crystal.

Phoenician bracelet. This gold piece of the seventh century BC was found on the Italian island of Sardinia.

DRINKING WATER
A large container on the aft guaranteed a one-day supply. As nightfall approached, the ship was anchored to the ground and refilled.

HOLDERS FOR OARS
This hollow pivot point gripped the oar and facilitated its rotation. The bireme included holders on the hull: circular holes coated with leather to prevent water from entering the ship.

The battle bireme

The naval battles and pirates forced the Phoenicians to build military ships, equipped with a ram at the bow to open waterways in other boats. To make them faster, the rows of rowers doubled and their number increased. Thus, the bireme was born.

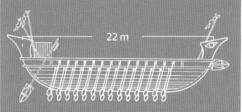

22 m

3.2 m

0.9 m

Stability. The open portholes in the hull lowered the gravity center of the ship. The almost horizontal position of the oar was more effective.

Power. The arrangement in two rows, with little separation between the deck and the hull, allowed the rowing to be performed by up to 60 men at a time.

SHELL
The planks that shaped ship (strakes) were joined together by rivets and butt straps and they were sewn to these flexible frames.

THE CELLAR
The pottery was fragile and could not be exposed to splashing, so it was stowed in the cellar. The stones acted as ballast to stabilize the boat.

OARS
Made of cedar wood, their distance to water was about 1.10 m. Trading ships had 8 to 12 oarsmen on each side.

The Greek trireme

Equipped with three rows of oars, the trireme gave the Greek fleet control of the Mediterranean for four centuries. Narrow, long, with a shallow draft and light, these ships stood out for their speed and maneuverability.

Hellenic naval hegemony

Since the beginning of the archaic era, in the eighth century BC, the main Greek cities seized the expertise of its sailors and the quality of their vessels to colonize the Mediterranean coast. From the sixth century BC, the threat of the Persian Empire forced the Greeks to develop a new warship based on the ancient penteconters used in the Trojan War. As the name suggests, the trireme had three banks of oars, arranged in different levels, allowing them to reach a speed never seen before.

TECHNICAL SHEET

▶ **Type:** Trireme galley
▶ **Crew:** 170 rowers and 14 soldiers.
▶ **Dimensions:**

25–32 m
Length

3.5–6 m
Beam

Oars layout

The arrangement of the rowers was one of the keys to the increased effectiveness of the Greek ships. In Phoenician vessels, the rowers of the higher row made a greater effort. The Greek triremes incorporated an outrigger, a protrusion of the hull, which facilitated work and did not increase the breadth of the vessel.

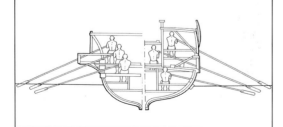

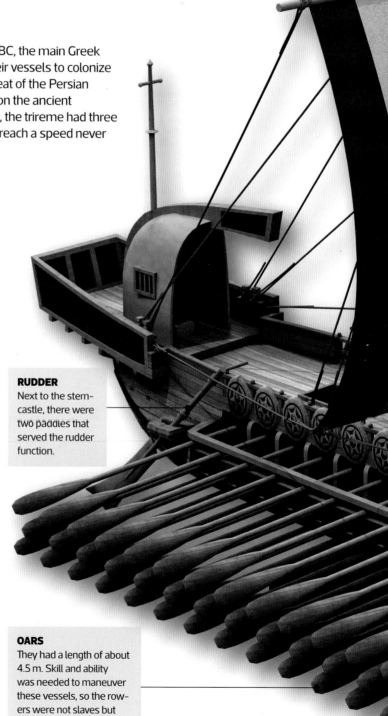

RUDDER
Next to the stern-castle, there were two paddles that served the rudder function.

OARS
They had a length of about 4.5 m. Skill and ability was needed to maneuver these vessels, so the rowers were not slaves but free citizens.

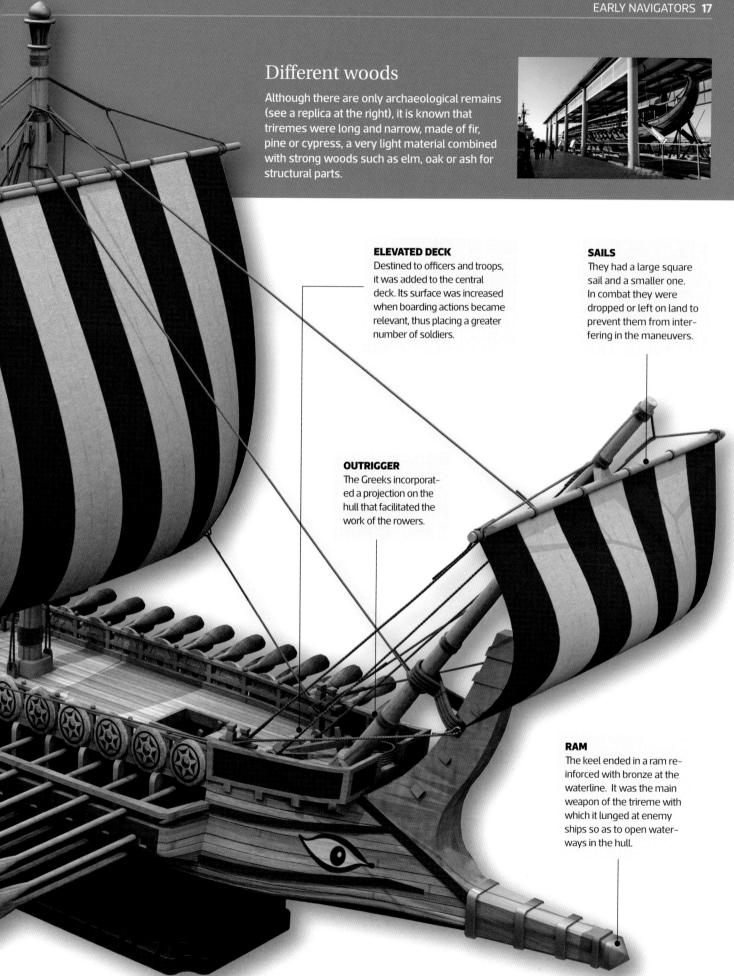

Different woods

Although there are only archaeological remains (see a replica at the right), it is known that triremes were long and narrow, made of fir, pine or cypress, a very light material combined with strong woods such as elm, oak or ash for structural parts.

ELEVATED DECK
Destined to officers and troops, it was added to the central deck. Its surface was increased when boarding actions became relevant, thus placing a greater number of soldiers.

SAILS
They had a large square sail and a smaller one. In combat they were dropped or left on land to prevent them from interfering in the maneuvers.

OUTRIGGER
The Greeks incorporated a projection on the hull that facilitated the work of the rowers.

RAM
The keel ended in a ram reinforced with bronze at the waterline. It was the main weapon of the trireme with which it lunged at enemy ships so as to open waterways in the hull.

The Roman galley

Although Rome did not invent the galleys, it was a maritime power with a large fleet of such ships. Built during the third century BC, they quickly gave the Romans a complete mastery of the Mediterranean.

Wind and brute force

The galley combined oars and sails , although if the wind was blowing against it, it could only rely on the strength of the rowers. Its rams and hooks to tie enemy ships proved to be feared weapons.

SAILS
Of square shape, they were only useful when the winds blew over the stern.

HULL
Constructed with soft woods such as pine and fir, very effective in the Mediterranean.

ARTIMON
Headsail characteristic of the galleys.

DATA SHEET
- **Crew:** 130 men, between rowers and other crew and soldiers.
- **Dimensions:** (a classic Liburnian with a Bireme setting).

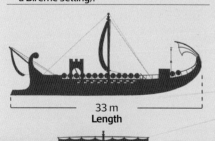

33 m
Length

8 m
Beam

RAM
Reinforced with metal and placed on the waterline, it was used to attack enemy ships.

CONNING TOWER
Roman contribution to the galley. From there, a hoist with hooks was handled that facilitated boarding actions.

CELLARS
Used to store food and other cargo.

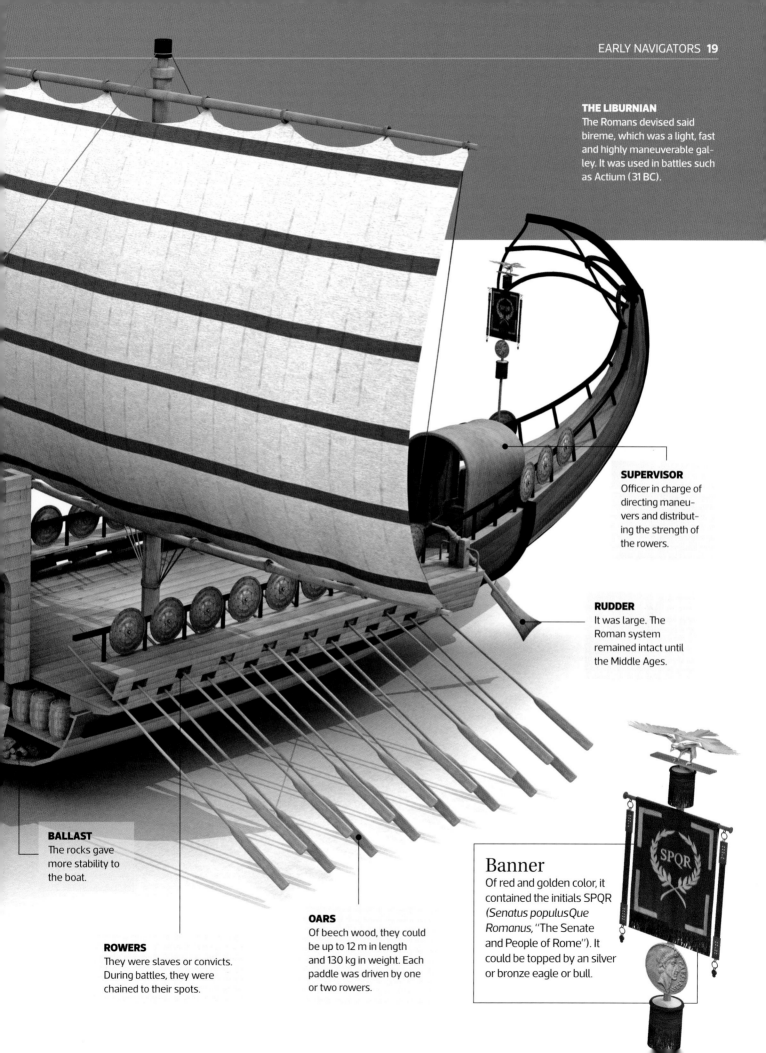

THE LIBURNIAN
The Romans devised said bireme, which was a light, fast and highly maneuverable galley. It was used in battles such as Actium (31 BC).

SUPERVISOR
Officer in charge of directing maneuvers and distributing the strength of the rowers.

RUDDER
It was large. The Roman system remained intact until the Middle Ages.

BALLAST
The rocks gave more stability to the boat.

ROWERS
They were slaves or convicts. During battles, they were chained to their spots.

OARS
Of beech wood, they could be up to 12 m in length and 130 kg in weight. Each paddle was driven by one or two rowers.

Banner
Of red and golden color, it contained the initials SPQR (*Senatus populusQue Romanus*, "The Senate and People of Rome"). It could be topped by an silver or bronze eagle or bull.

The Arab dhow

When this little vessel of Arab origin began to sail the seas, it represented a revolutionary innovation: triangular sails that allowed navigating without rowers, as they did not require tailwind.

Ambassador of a new faith

There are no certainties about it, but many historians argue that the dhow, designed as a cargo vessel, was one of the keys to the overwhelming expansion of Islam through the Mediterranean Sea and the Indian Ocean, as from the seventh century. At present, the construction of these vessels continues, which has hardly been altered in 1300 years.

MAST
The dhows could have between one and three. It is possible that the first ones were made of coconut palms.

ROPES
They were made from coconut palm fibers.

RUDDER
Generally small in relation to the vessel, it was appropriate to sail with strong winds.

TECHNICAL SHEET
▸ **Type:** Freighter
▸ **Crew:** 15–30
▸ **Dimensions:**

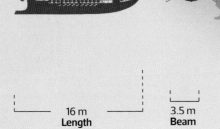

16 m
Length

3.5 m
Beam

JOINTS
Other distinguishing feature of the dhow was that its hull components were joined by ropes, fibers and belts.

HULL
Made of wood, its lines may have served as a model for subsequent galleys and caravels.

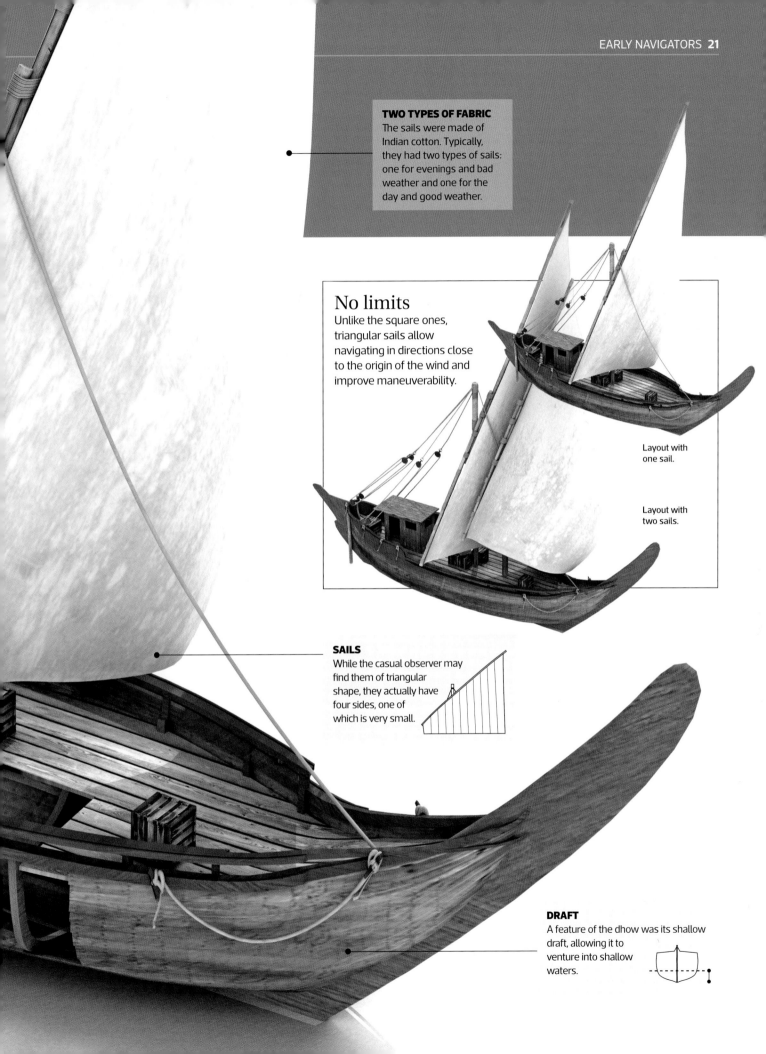

TWO TYPES OF FABRIC
The sails were made of
Indian cotton. Typically,
they had two types of sails:
one for evenings and bad
weather and one for the
day and good weather.

No limits

Unlike the square ones,
triangular sails allow
navigating in directions close
to the origin of the wind and
improve maneuverability.

Layout with
one sail.

Layout with
two sails.

SAILS
While the casual observer may
find them of triangular
shape, they actually have
four sides, one of
which is very small.

DRAFT
A feature of the dhow was its shallow
draft, allowing it to
venture into shallow
waters.

The Viking ship

The Vikings were a people of great sailors who dominated the sea routes and the rivers in north-western Europe between the eighth and eleventh centuries, reaching even some parts of the Mediterranean coast, with their peculiar light ships.

Trade and War

Basically, the Vikings had two types of boat. For their war raids and looting, they used a long, light and narrow vessel, the drekar, while a wider and flatter version of it (the knarr), was used for trade, which was especially designed for transporting wood, wool, skins, wheat or even slaves. The lightness of these vessels reached the point where the crew could easily drag them to the edge and beyond, sometimes transporting them across fields from one river to another.

TECHNICAL SHEET

▶ **Type:** Boat with lashed hull
▶ **Crew:** Up to 30 soldiers
▶ **Dimensions:**

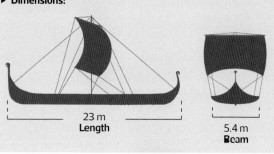

23 m
Length

5.4 m
Beam

SAIL
It had a single square sail of about 10 meters per side, made of linen or wool.

OARS
There were 16 pairs. When sailing, the oars were collected on trestles with a "T" shape.

FIGUREHEAD
Being skilled craftsmen, the Vikings carved on wood an emblematic animal, a mix between a dragon and snake tangled on itself.

KEEL
A stout one-piece oaken keel of over 25 m gave great strength to the ship and allowed to navigate with just one meter of water.

Gokstad ship

The discovery, in 1880, of the Gokstad ship in southern Norway allowed progress in the knowledge we have today about the Vikings. This drekar dates from about 900 AD, it is over 23 meters long and its weight, including the rigging, is about 20 tonnes.

"DREKI"
The figure carved into the bow, besides frightening enemies, was used as a sort of amulet to ward off evil spirits.

RUDDER
It was placed on the stern, starboard, fixed to the gunwale with a leather strap. Over time, the rudder became increasingly wider.

Background

Fishing activity in the Scandinavian coastline favored shipbuilding. See its evolution, known through different archaeological findings (ship remains and drawings and relief on flat stones).

Neolithic Canoe, towards 3500 BC.

Hjortspring boat, towards 350 BC.

Halsenoy boat, towards 100 AD.

Nydam boat, towards 350 AD.

Kvalsund boat, towards 700 AD.

HULL
The bottom boards measured only 2.6 cm. The tenth row had to be the strongest (4.3 cm) since it was located at the waterline.

LOAD
Being war ships, the drekar allowed little cargo. On the contrary, the knarr, boats engaged in trade, could even carry cattle on the deck.

The Hanseatic cog

One of the most powerful alliances in the Middle Ages was the Hanseatic League, formed by cities of the North Sea and Baltic Sea, which had special status to trade between them. The cog was, in this sense, the "soul" of trade in the League.

The Queen of the North

A large sail, spacious cellars and adaptations to navigate stormy waters turned the cog into the queens of the northern seas during the fourteenth century. One of its most important innovations was probably the rudder on the center of the stern.

TOP
It was a privileged watching position; however, from said place not only vertigo had to be endured, but also the constant wobbling of the ship.

FORECASTLE
It is assumed that this structure, that was richly ornamented in general, was used for surveillance purposes, and to facilitate boarding actions.

RUDDER
The oldest cogs had a Nordic-type rudder with paddles on both sides of the stern. Since the fourteenth century, only one has been placed on the middle of the stern.

HULL
It had an elongated shape, similar to that of former Norman boats.

KEEL
Long and straight, it was suitable to face bad weather conditions in the North Sea.

TECHNICAL SHEET

▶ **Type:** Coca
▶ **Crew:** Unknown
▶ **Dimensions:**

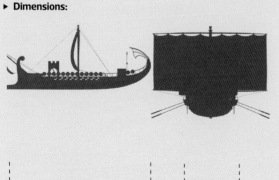

30 m
Length

8 m
Beam

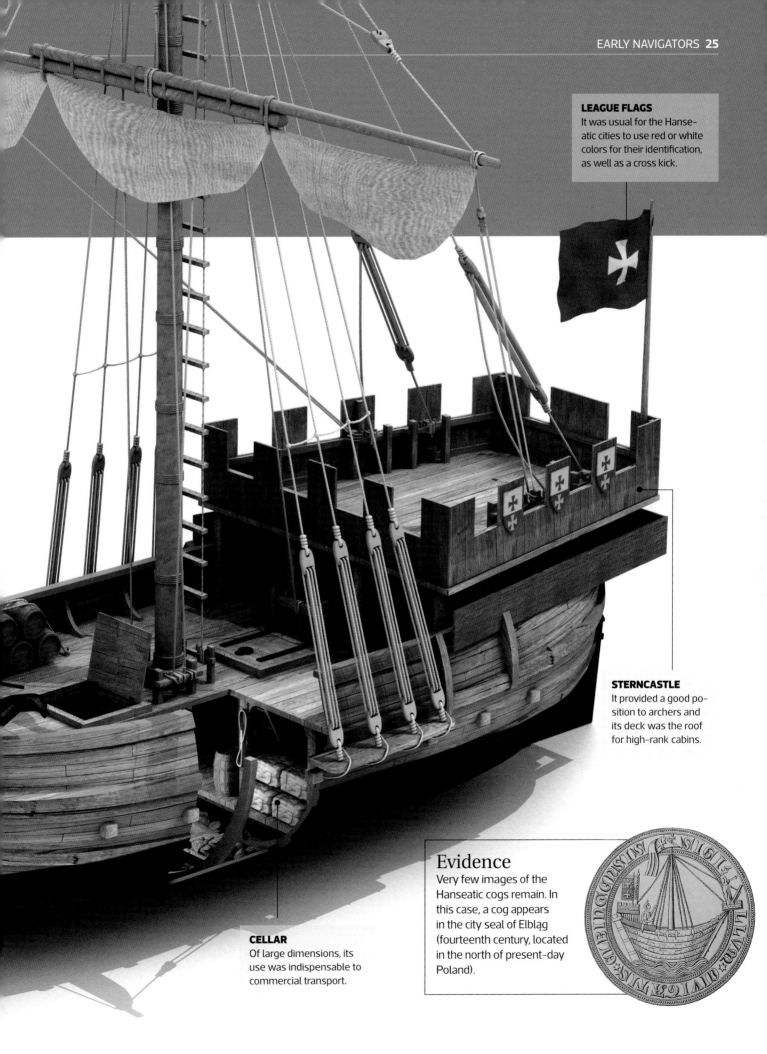

LEAGUE FLAGS
It was usual for the Hanse-atic cities to use red or white colors for their identification, as well as a cross kick.

STERNCASTLE
It provided a good po-sition to archers and its deck was the roof for high-rank cabins.

CELLAR
Of large dimensions, its use was indispensable to commercial transport.

Evidence
Very few images of the Hanseatic cogs remain. In this case, a cog appears in the city seal of Elbląg (fourteenth century, located in the north of present-day Poland).

The Byzantine dromon

The dromon was the Byzantine warship prototype between the sixth and thirteenth centuries. Over time, these ships (designed to be fast) increased their size and improved their rig.

Floating arsenal

The iconic dromons of the Byzantine navy, propelled by the wind and the strength of over a hundred rowers, were feared for their deadly weapons. They counted with rams, platforms for archers, ballistae, catapults and bronze siphons that, like flamethrowers, projected the devastating "Greek fire."

SAILS
Sails could be square or lateen, or a combination of the two.

MASTS
It is believed that the larger dromons required two or three masts (one sail would have to be too large).

THE "GREEK FIRE"
It was a flammable and explosive mixture potentially consisting of naphtha, quicklime, sulphur and pitch, which was not extinguished with water. It was projected through a siphon mechanism, similar to a modern flamethrower.

FORECASTLE
Elevated above the deck, it was designed to shoot from there the "Greek fire."

RAM
Designed for boarding actions, the dromon was provided with a bow ram that served to break the oars and flanks of the enemy ships.

HULL
Made of wood, with transverse reinforcement.

MIDDLE CASTLE
Located around the main mast, it probably served as a platform for archers.

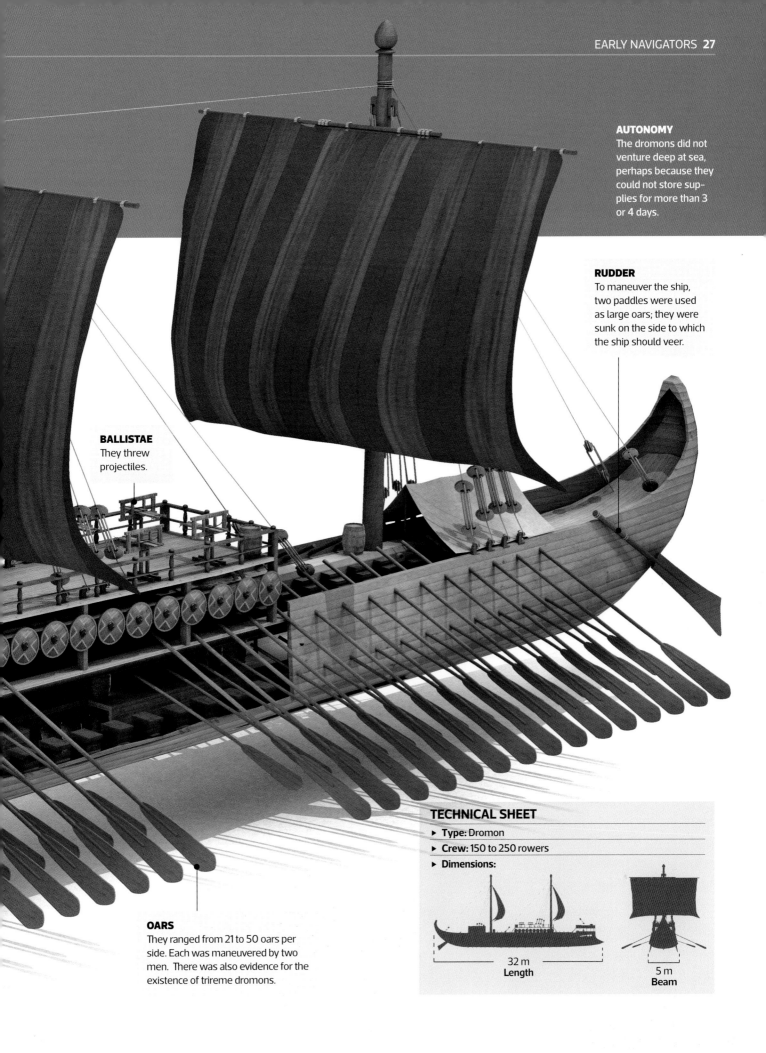

AUTONOMY
The dromons did not venture deep at sea, perhaps because they could not store supplies for more than 3 or 4 days.

RUDDER
To maneuver the ship, two paddles were used as large oars; they were sunk on the side to which the ship should veer.

BALLISTAE
They threw projectiles.

OARS
They ranged from 21 to 50 oars per side. Each was maneuvered by two men. There was also evidence for the existence of trireme dromons.

TECHNICAL SHEET
▸ **Type:** Dromon
▸ **Crew:** 150 to 250 rowers
▸ **Dimensions:**

32 m
Length

5 m
Beam

Zheng He's fleet

Six centuries ago, the Indian Ocean witnessed the passage of a formidable fleet of over 300 ships. It was under the command of the Chinese admiral Zheng He.

The "treasure ships"

That was the name (in Chinese, *bao suchuan*) of the most luxurious ships of all those that accompanied Zheng He on seven major maritime expeditions. There are almost no traces of these huge ships sent by the Chinese Emperor in the fifteenth century to explore and trade outside the empire.

TECHNICAL SHEET

▸ **Crew:** The fleet was made up of about 30,000 men in over 300 ships.
▸ **Dimensions:** It is believed that the "treasure ships" were over 100 m long and 40 m wide, although no ship has been kept.

ZHENG HE
Famous admiral that served the Ming Dynasty, Zheng He was a eunuch of Muslim origin. He led seven expeditions over 28 years.

CRANES
They were used to load and unload the ship.

SAILS
Nine masts held huge sails, reinforced with bamboo.

ANCHORS
They were made of iron. They were more than two meters long.

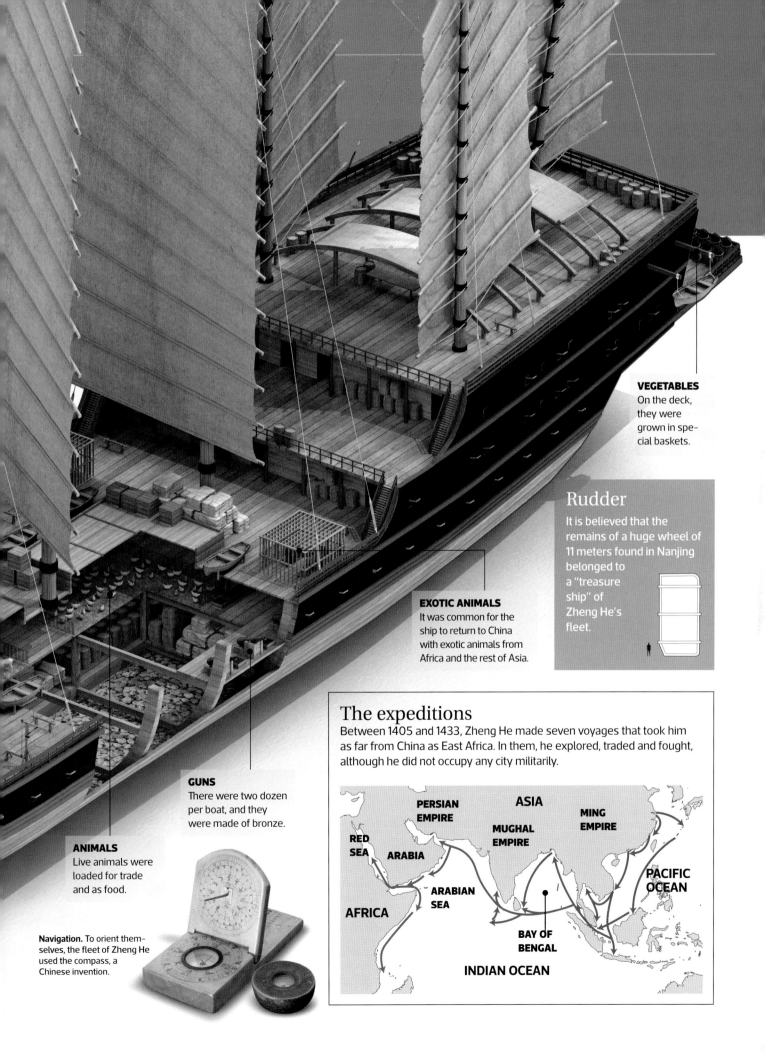

VEGETABLES
On the deck, they were grown in special baskets.

Rudder

It is believed that the remains of a huge wheel of 11 meters found in Nanjing belonged to a "treasure ship" of Zheng He's fleet.

EXOTIC ANIMALS
It was common for the ship to return to China with exotic animals from Africa and the rest of Asia.

GUNS
There were two dozen per boat, and they were made of bronze.

ANIMALS
Live animals were loaded for trade and as food.

Navigation. To orient themselves, the fleet of Zheng He used the compass, a Chinese invention.

The expeditions

Between 1405 and 1433, Zheng He made seven voyages that took him as far from China as East Africa. In them, he explored, traded and fought, although he did not occupy any city militarily.

PERSIAN EMPIRE

ASIA

MUGHAL EMPIRE

MING EMPIRE

RED SEA

ARABIA

ARABIAN SEA

AFRICA

BAY OF BENGAL

PACIFIC OCEAN

INDIAN OCEAN

The caravels

These iconic sail boats dominated the Atlantic in the fifteenth and sixteenth centuries. Jointly with the carracks, they allowed the passage of coastal sailing to ocean navigation and the discovery of a new world across the ocean.

The ship of discovery

The lightweight and fast caravels, widely used by Portuguese navigators during the fifteenth century, were certainly suitable vessels for transoceanic adventures, such as those that led the Genovese navigator Christopher Columbus to the Americas. Lower and more maneuverable than the carracks (the other large ships of that time), the caravels used triangular lateen sails, but they could also have square sails. Eventually, they fell into disuse against the galleons, an evolution of the carracks.

SAILS
The caravels carried lateen sails, but they were usually combined with square sails (rounded caravels) to harness the wind from the aft.

FORECASTLE
This elevated structure, useful for defence, housed the foremast and bowsprit (the tilted mast, with spritsail).

CROSS OF SAINT JAMES
It was common in Spanish caravels since Santiago was the patron of the country. He was invoked for a good weather.

HULL
The gaskets used to open and cause irreparable water leaks. Many caravels were dismantled upon reaching ports after making long voyages.

TECHNICAL SHEET

▸ **Type:** Caravel

▸ **Crew:** Between 25 and 40 sailors

▸ **Dimensions:**

30 m
Length

8 m
Beam

Replicas of Columbus' ships

There are several replicas of the three ships that Columbus used to reach America, though in his Logbook he calls the *Santa Maria* a carrack, like those exhibited in La Rabida (Palos de la Frontera, Spain), the departure point of the famous voyage to the Americas.

BOMBARDS AND FALCONETS
The caravels could carry these small pieces of artillery. In addition, the crew had other weapons like culverins, springalds and crossbows.

CAPTAIN CABIN
When Columbus moved to *La Niña*, he ordered the construction of a cabin on the aft quarter-deck of the caravel.

ANCHORS
They used to carry four anchors, which came up with a capstan or vertical lathe.

CELLAR
It was large (with a capacity of about 50 tons) since it had to store enough food for overseas travel. They also carried animals.

The *Victoria*

Emblem of the first fleet that managed to go around the world, led by Portuguese navigator Ferdinand Magellan, the *Victoria* incorporated technological advances that opened the door to the great discoveries of the sixteenth century.

More masts and sails

Heirs of the technical advances of the cogs, the carracks incorporated more masts, they possessed a large freeboard and they had both a forecastle and an aftcastle. In general, the carracks were propelled by large square sails, though later some combinations with triangular sails appeared.

TECHNICAL SHEET

▶ **Type:** Carrack
▶ **Crew:** 42
▶ **Dimensions::**

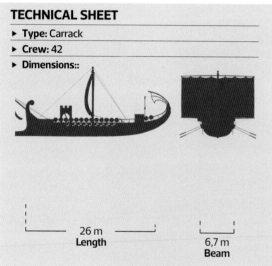

26 m
Length

6,7 m
Beam

Maneuverability

For centuries, ships were maneuvered with a paddle rudder (a kind of large oar placed on the side it was necessary to turn), which was much more rudimentary. In the carracks, the stern rudder offered greater maneuverability.

MASTS
Unlike the cogs, which only had one mast, the carracks had three masts, and a bowsprit as well.

SAIL AREA
The six linen sails of the *Victoria* totalled an area of approximately 290 m².

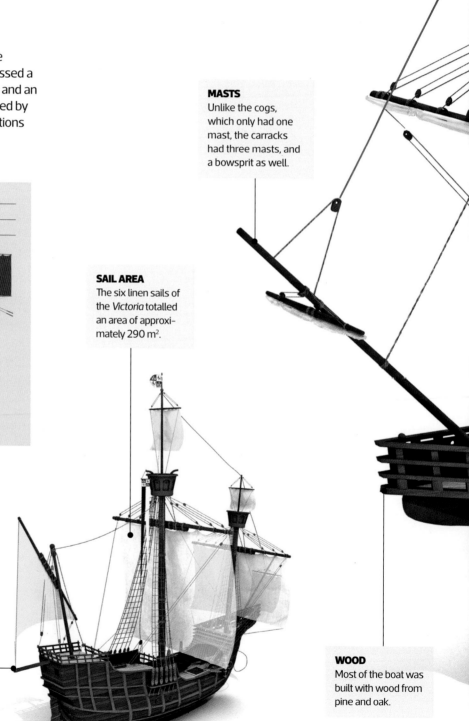

STERN RUDDER
This vertical movable part was located at the stern as an extension of the keel.

WOOD
Most of the boat was built with wood from pine and oak.

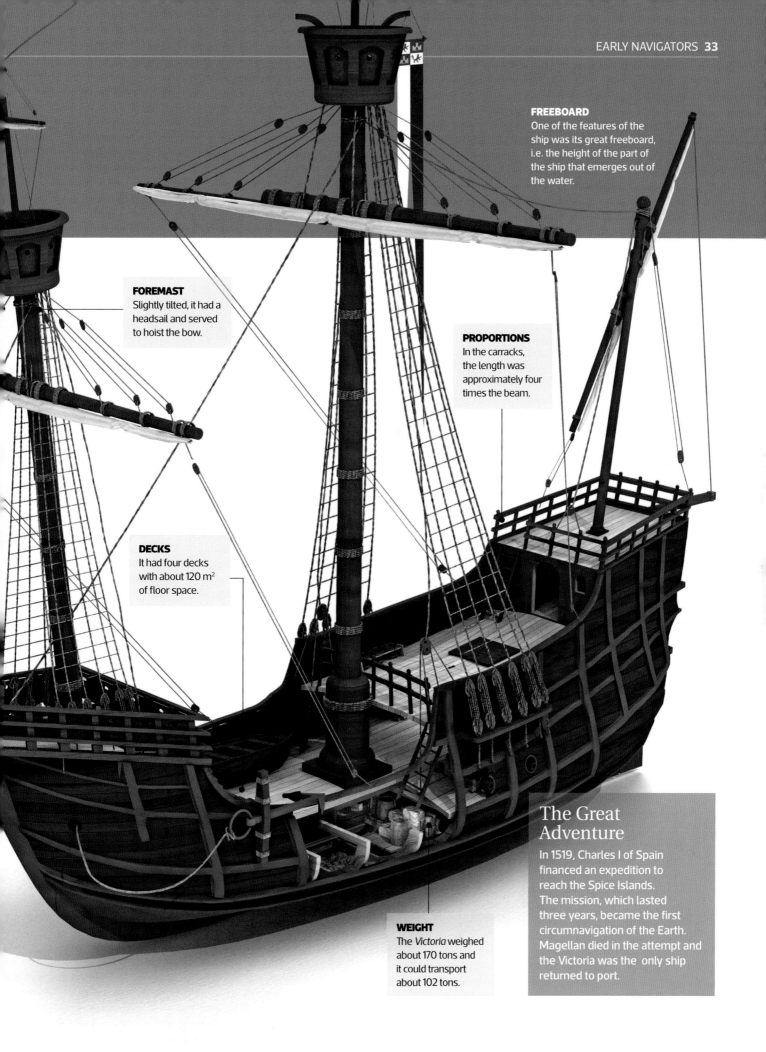

FREEBOARD
One of the features of the ship was its great freeboard, i.e. the height of the part of the ship that emerges out of the water.

FOREMAST
Slightly tilted, it had a headsail and served to hoist the bow.

PROPORTIONS
In the carracks, the length was approximately four times the beam.

DECKS
It had four decks with about 120 m² of floor space.

WEIGHT
The *Victoria* weighed about 170 tons and it could transport about 102 tons.

The Great Adventure

In 1519, Charles I of Spain financed an expedition to reach the Spice Islands. The mission, which lasted three years, became the first circumnavigation of the Earth. Magellan died in the attempt and the Victoria was the only ship returned to port.

Exploring the world

In the fifteenth century, the compass and sextant, greater geographical and astronomical knowledge and the reading of ancient texts and writings of Arab travellers encouraged sailors to find new trade routes to the East by the Atlantic.

The age of discovery

Prince Henry the Navigator of Portugal founded in Sagres the first naval school in the world and soon the Portuguese sailors occupied the islands of Madeira, Azores and Cape Verde. Bartolomeu Dias went around the Cape of Good Hope, and Vasco da Gama opened the Indian Ocean route. A few years before, Christopher Columbus came across the American continent searching to reach India by the west. With these trips, two great empires were born: the Spanish Empire in America and the Portuguese Empire in Africa and India, to which the Treaty of Tordesillas added Brazil. Magellan, Portuguese explorer that served Castile, began the expedition around the world completed by Juan Sebastian Elcano. Also, the new routes were explored by British, French and Dutch sailors, such as the Cabot brothers, Jacques Cartier or Francis Drake.

New horizons

In the fifteenth century, Portuguese sailors began a new era of transoceanic navigation that allowed reaching all the corners of the world and led to the creation of great empires.

1 The Portuguese precursors
The Portuguese arrive in Madeira (1420) and the Azores islands (1427). Diego Cao explores the Congo River (1482). Bartolomeu Dias goes around Cape of Good Hope (1487).

2 The voyages of Columbus
Columbus' first voyage (1492): Guanahani, Cuba and Santo Domingo. Three new trips in 1493, 1498 and 1502. Treaty of Tordesillas (1494). Portuguese Empire in India (1492).

3 Exploring travellers
Magellan undertakes the first round the world (1510). Núñez de Balboa discovers the Pacific (1513). The Dutch Tasman reached Tasmania, New Zealand and New Guinea (1642).

4 Scientific expeditions
Bougainville explores Melanesia and Polynesia (1766). First trip around the world by James Cook (1768). Trip by German scientist von Humboldt (1799-1804).

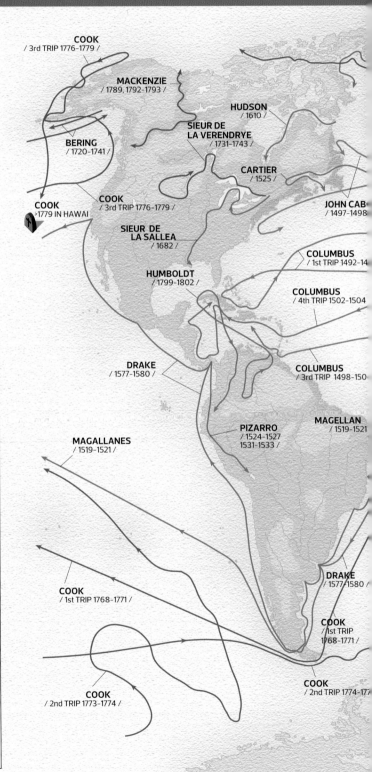

COOK / 3rd TRIP 1776-1779 /

MACKENZIE / 1789, 1792-1793 /

HUDSON / 1610 /

SIEUR DE LA VERENDRYE / 1731-1743 /

BERING / 1720-1741 /

CARTIER / 1525 /

COOK >1779 IN HAWAI

COOK / 3rd TRIP 1776-1779 /

JOHN CABOT / 1497-1498 /

SIEUR DE LA SALLEA / 1682 /

COLUMBUS / 1st TRIP 1492-14

HUMBOLDT / 1799-1802 /

COLUMBUS / 4th TRIP 1502-1504

COLUMBUS / 3rd TRIP 1498-150

DRAKE / 1577-1580 /

COLUMBUS / 3rd TRIP 1498-150

MAGELLAN / 1519-1521 /

PIZARRO / 1524-1527 1531-1533 /

MAGALLANES / 1519-1521 /

DRAKE / 1577-1580 /

COOK / 1st TRIP 1768-1771 /

COOK / 1st TRIP 1768-1771 /

COOK / 2nd TRIP 1774-17

COOK / 2nd TRIP 1773-1774 /

Captain James Cook

The three voyages of James Cook on the Endeavour allowed him to explore the islands in the Pacific Ocean and the coasts of Australia and New Zealand, the sought *Terra Australis*. Cook provided the Royal Society with valuable scientific data, sailed in the Antarctic Ocean, took two trips around the world and sought an Arctic passage between the Atlantic and the Pacific Oceans.

NAUTICAL ASTROLABE

As from the sixteenth century, the development and improvement of technical navigational instruments facilitated the piloting of ships.

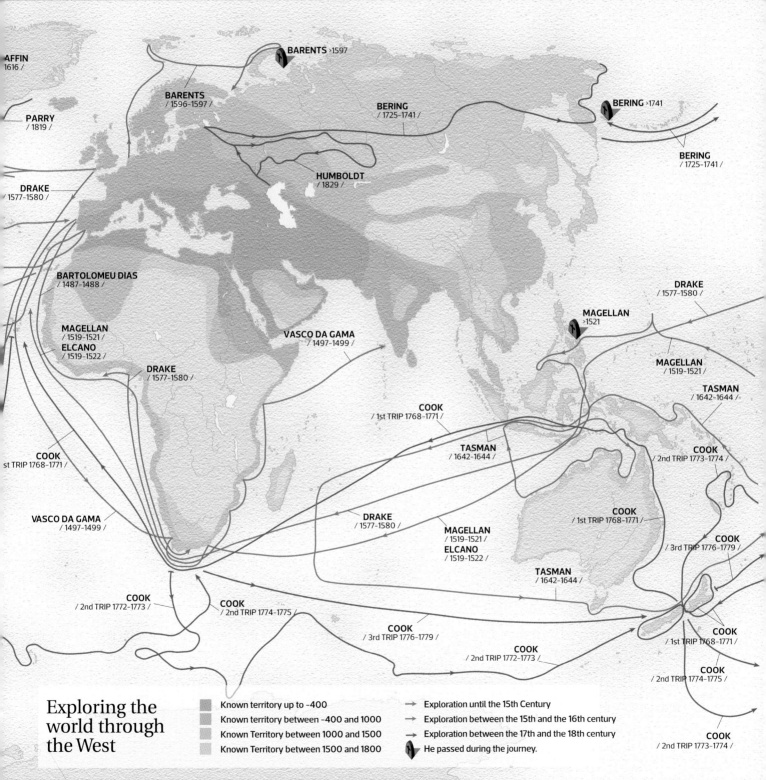

AFFIN
1616 /

BARENTS ›1597

PARRY
/ 1819 /

BARENTS
/ 1596–1597 /

BERING
/ 1725–1741 /

BERING ›1741

DRAKE
/ 1577–1580 /

HUMBOLDT
/ 1829 /

BERING
/ 1725–1741 /

BARTOLOMEU DIAS
/ 1487–1488 /

DRAKE
/ 1577–1580 /

MAGELLAN
/ 1519–1521 /
ELCANO
/ 1519–1522 /

VASCO DA GAMA
/ 1497–1499 /

MAGELLAN
›1521

DRAKE
/ 1577–1580 /

MAGELLAN
/ 1519–1521 /

TASMAN
/ 1642–1644 /

COOK
/ 1st TRIP 1768–1771 /

COOK
/ 2nd TRIP 1773–1774 /

TASMAN
/ 1642–1644 /

COOK
st TRIP 1768–1771 /

COOK
/ 1st TRIP 1768–1771 /

COOK
/ 3rd TRIP 1776–1779 /

VASCO DA GAMA
/ 1497–1499 /

DRAKE
/ 1577–1580 /

MAGELLAN
/ 1519–1521 /
ELCANO
/ 1519–1522 /

TASMAN
/ 1642–1644 /

COOK
/ 1st TRIP 1768–1771 /

COOK
/ 2nd TRIP 1772–1773 /

COOK
/ 2nd TRIP 1774–1775 /

COOK
/ 3rd TRIP 1776–1779 /

COOK
/ 2nd TRIP 1772–1773 /

COOK
/ 2nd TRIP 1774–1775 /

COOK
/ 2nd TRIP 1773–1774 /

Exploring the world through the West

- Known territory up to –400
- Known territory between –400 and 1000
- Known Territory between 1000 and 1500
- Known Territory between 1500 and 1800

→ Exploration until the 15th Century
→ Exploration between the 15th and the 16th century
→ Exploration between the 17th and the 18th century

He passed during the journey.

From sail to steam

Chapter 2

After the discovery of America, the major maritime powers endowed their powerful fleets with galleons and galleys to carry and protect the wealth from the new colonies. Meanwhile, piracy became the scourge of the newly created trade routes, especially in the Caribbean. Great expeditions were organized to settle the new lands, such as the one starred by Pilgrims aboard the English ship *Mayflower*.

In the late eighteenth century, the Industrial Revolution represented a key impulse in the history of navigation as steam engines were incorporated (in 1819, the *Savannah* managed to cross the Atlantic powered in this way), as well as the propeller and new materials such as iron and, subsequently, steel for the manufacture of the hulls. The first successful submarine trials were also conducted. At this stage, great naval engineers shone with their own light, such as Robert Felton, Robert Seppings or Isambard K. Brunel.

In short, the new advances enabled the manufacture of ships with greater capacity and better performance at all levels, designed to successfully tackle the transoceanic trade routes of the time. As for the navy, in the second half of the nineteenth century, battleships started turning into reference vessels.

Galleys

In the fifteenth and sixteenth centuries, the galleys, long, fast and maneuverable ships with shallow draft were the most powerful war ships in the Mediterranean. *La Réale*, commanded by Don John of Austria at the Battle of Lepanto, was one of the most famous galleys.

Flagship in Lepanto

The galley was a proportionally very long boat that combined sailing and rowing, the design of which dates back to the ancient Mediterranean. Eventually, it incorporated more rowers and, in the sixteenth century, models began to be built with a foremost mast or foremast that displaced the main mast to a more central position. *La Réale*, built in 1568, was the largest galley of its time. With Don Juan de Austria in command, it was the flagship of the Spanish fleet in the Battle of Lepanto, in which the ships of the Holy League defeated the Ottoman fleet of Uluj Ali.

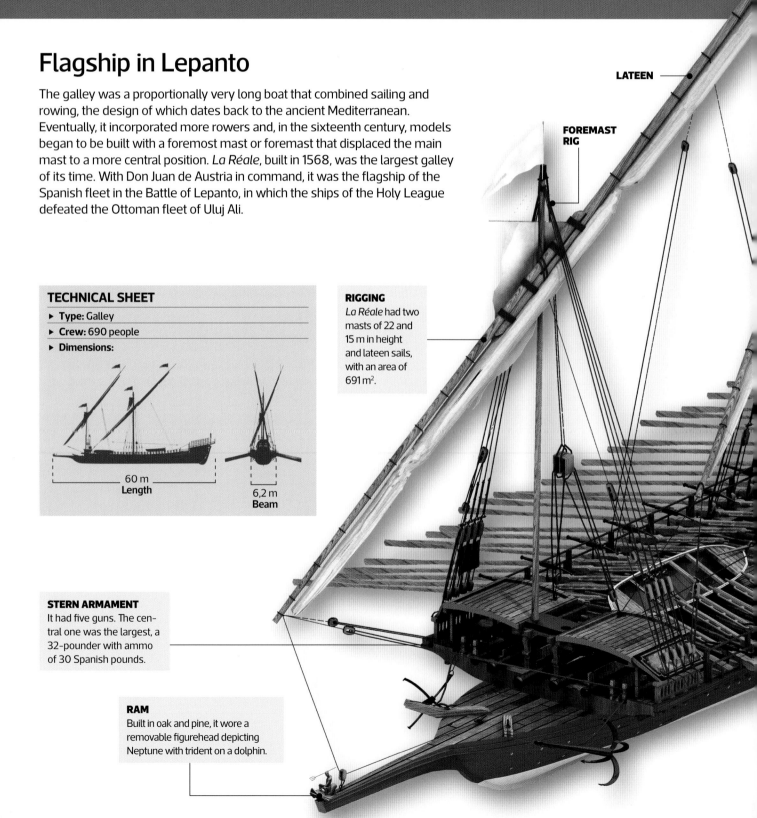

TECHNICAL SHEET

▶ **Type:** Galley
▶ **Crew:** 690 people
▶ **Dimensions:**

60 m
Length

6,2 m
Beam

LATEEN

FOREMAST RIG

RIGGING
La Réale had two masts of 22 and 15 m in height and lateen sails, with an area of 691 m².

STERN ARMAMENT
It had five guns. The central one was the largest, a 32-pounder with ammo of 30 Spanish pounds.

RAM
Built in oak and pine, it wore a removable figurehead depicting Neptune with trident on a dolphin.

Aft float

As it was home to a member of the royal family, the entire exterior was richly ornamented with bas-reliefs and sculptures, many of them with religious themes and mythological figures and scenes combined with symbols of Catholic dogma.

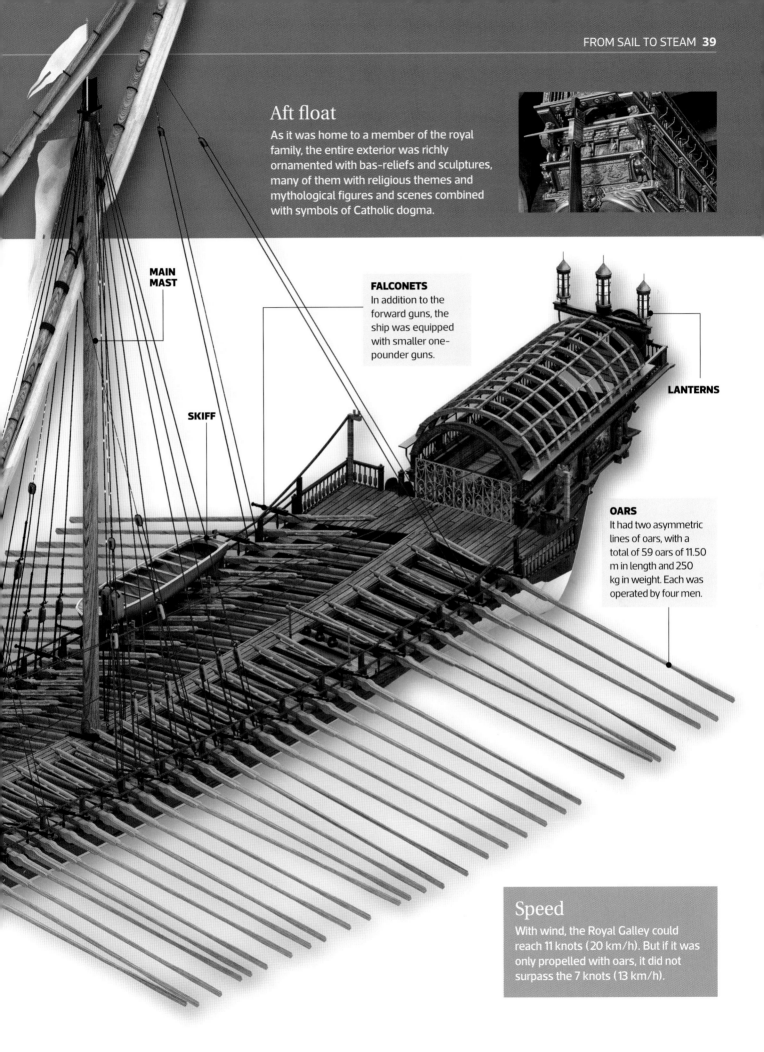

MAIN MAST

FALCONETS
In addition to the forward guns, the ship was equipped with smaller one-pounder guns.

LANTERNS

SKIFF

OARS
It had two asymmetric lines of oars, with a total of 59 oars of 11.50 m in length and 250 kg in weight. Each was operated by four men.

Speed

With wind, the Royal Galley could reach 11 knots (20 km/h). But if it was only propelled with oars, it did not surpass the 7 knots (13 km/h).

Korean turtle ship

The "turtle ships" or *Geobukseon* date from the early fifteenth century, but the final design is attributed to Admiral Yi Sun-sin who ordered its construction to repel the Japanese invasion of Korea in 1592-1598.

Eastern sea fortress

The *Geobukseon* were strong and stable, but also light, fast and highly maneuverable ships. According to the notes in the War Diary of its builder, Yi Sun-sin, these vessels were equipped with powerful artillery and the rowers were protected by an armor plate with spikes, which gave the ship an aspect similar to a turtle, hence its nickname. For some historians, these are considered the first battleships in history.

SAILS
There were two sails reinforced with numerous rods that gave them great strength. In combat, masts and sails could be removed.

TECHNICAL SHEET

▸ **Type:** Panokseon
▸ **Crew:** 130 (70-80 rowers and 50-60 soldiers)
▸ **Dimensions:**

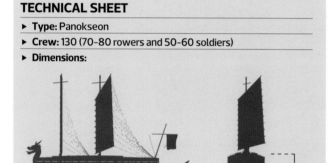

7 m

33 m
Length

DRAGON-SHAPED HEAD
Although according to the drawings of the eighteenth century, it was situated as a stood as a figurehead (similar to Chinese dragon boats), new research determined that it was likely located at the waterline, as a battering ram.

SPIKES
The shell was covered with metal spikes to prevent boarding actions.

SHELL
Made of hexagonal plates, it covered the main deck and it has not been determined whether it was made of iron or wood.

ANCHOR
Made of wood and of a large size, it was another hallmark of this type of ship.

Yi Sun-sin (1545-1598)

Korean admiral, famous commissioning the construction in 1592 several "turtle ship" from some old blueprints. Using a small fleet, he defended his country's from repeated conquer attempts of the Japanese. He died from a shot in a battle against the Japanese enemy.

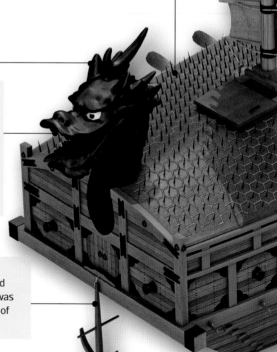

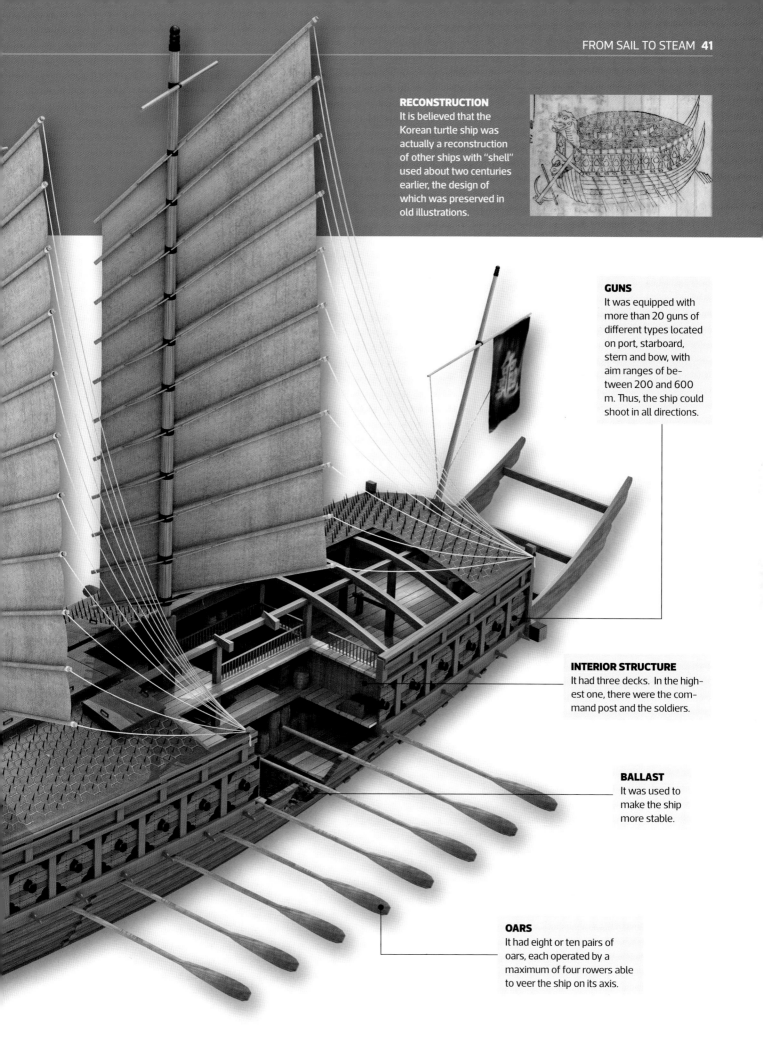

RECONSTRUCTION
It is believed that the Korean turtle ship was actually a reconstruction of other ships with "shell" used about two centuries earlier, the design of which was preserved in old illustrations.

GUNS
It was equipped with more than 20 guns of different types located on port, starboard, stern and bow, with aim ranges of between 200 and 600 m. Thus, the ship could shoot in all directions.

INTERIOR STRUCTURE
It had three decks. In the highest one, there were the command post and the soldiers.

BALLAST
It was used to make the ship more stable.

OARS
It had eight or ten pairs of oars, each operated by a maximum of four rowers able to veer the ship on its axis.

Galleons

The galleons were powerful vessels with high load and combat capacity prepared to tackle transoceanic routes. They constituted the bulk of the major European fleets in the sixteenth and seventeenth centuries.

Trade with the colonies

Galleons transited the transoceanic route in fleets organized for self-defence. Although Spain was the country that made this tactic famous, other countries also adopted it: Portugal did it in the sixteenth century (to trade slaves for wood and sugar in Brazil) and England in the seventeenth century (to import snuff from Virginia). One of the most important galleons was *Nuestra Señora de Atocha* ("Our Lady of Atocha") (see image) that sank in 1622 off the Florida Keys due to a hurricane with a valuable cargo on board.

TECHNICAL SHEET

- ▶ **Type:** Galleon
- ▶ **Crew:** 265 (sailors, officers and soldiers)
- ▶ **Dimensions:**

34 m
Length

10 m
Beam

The treasure

The *Nuestra Señora de Atocha* sank with 24 t of silver bullion, 500 kg of emeralds and pearls, 707 gold and copper ingots, 180,000 silver coins and numerous artefacts and jewellery of great value. The treasure was salvaged 364 years after her shipwreck.

FOREMOST MAST

SAILS

The sails were square for the main mast and for the fore-most mast to take advantage of favorable winds, and she had a lateen on the mizzen. The galleons were faster than the caravels, despite having lesser length.

CULVERIN

Located in the castles, these cannons were cast in one piece. They used to be between 1 and 3 m long and they fired small caliber cannon balls.

BOW

She had a forecastle and an aftercastle and the ram lost its offensive role.

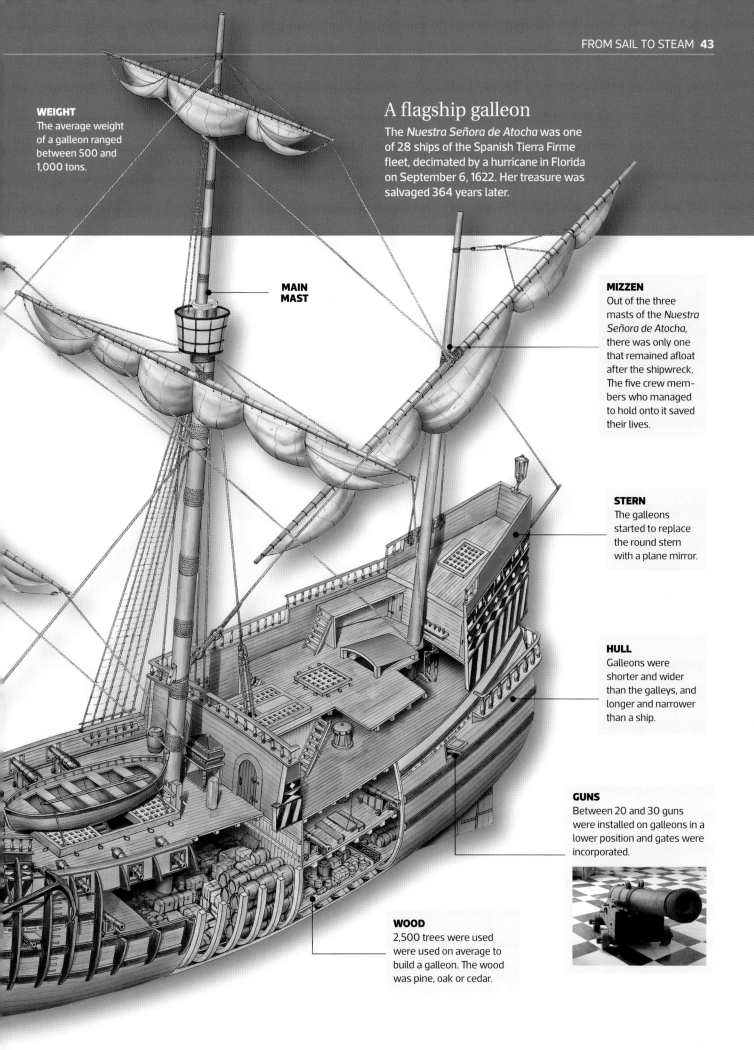

WEIGHT
The average weight of a galleon ranged between 500 and 1,000 tons.

A flagship galleon

The *Nuestra Señora de Atocha* was one of 28 ships of the Spanish Tierra Firme fleet, decimated by a hurricane in Florida on September 6, 1622. Her treasure was salvaged 364 years later.

MAIN MAST

MIZZEN
Out of the three masts of the *Nuestra Señora de Atocha*, there was only one that remained afloat after the shipwreck. The five crew members who managed to hold onto it saved their lives.

STERN
The galleons started to replace the round stern with a plane mirror.

HULL
Galleons were shorter and wider than the galleys, and longer and narrower than a ship.

GUNS
Between 20 and 30 guns were installed on galleons in a lower position and gates were incorporated.

WOOD
2,500 trees were used were used on average to build a galleon. The wood was pine, oak or cedar.

The *Mayflower*

On September 16, 1620, a hundred men, including religious separatists and adventurers, left England for the New World with the intention of founding a colony. The so-called Pilgrims arrived in America 66 days later.

The "May Flower"

Initially, the trip to America was planned in two ships, the *Mayflower* and the *Speedwell*. But as soon as they left the port, the *Speedwell* suffered a major failure that forced her to return. All passengers had to move to the *Mayflower*. Although there are no records that describe the characteristics of this boat, her reconstruction was possible by considering merchant ships that sailed the seas with similar tonnage in the late sixteenth century.

Rigging

The ship had three masts and six sails the movement of which was controlled by a set of 55 strings, manipulated by the crew under the command of an officer.

TECHNICAL SHEET
- ▸ **Type:** Galley
- ▸ **Crew:** 25 men
- ▸ **Dimensions:**

7.6 m
Beam

33.5 m
Length

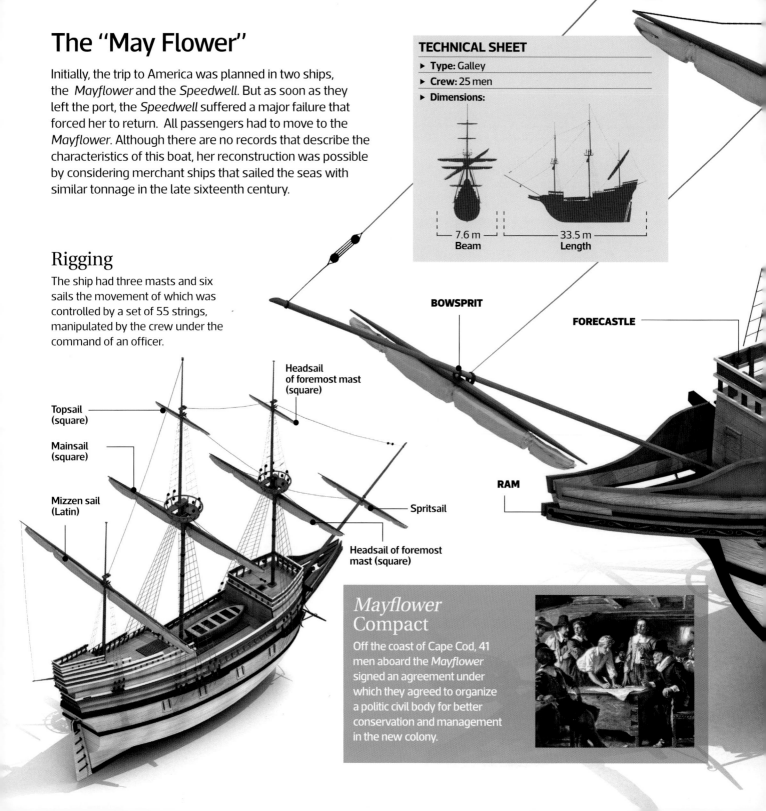

BOWSPRIT

FORECASTLE

Headsail
of foremost mast
(square)

Topsail
(square)

Mainsail
(square)

Mizzen sail
(Latin)

Spritsail

RAM

Headsail of foremost
mast (square)

Mayflower Compact

Off the coast of Cape Cod, 41 men aboard the *Mayflower* signed an agreement under which they agreed to organize a politic civil body for better conservation and management in the new colony.

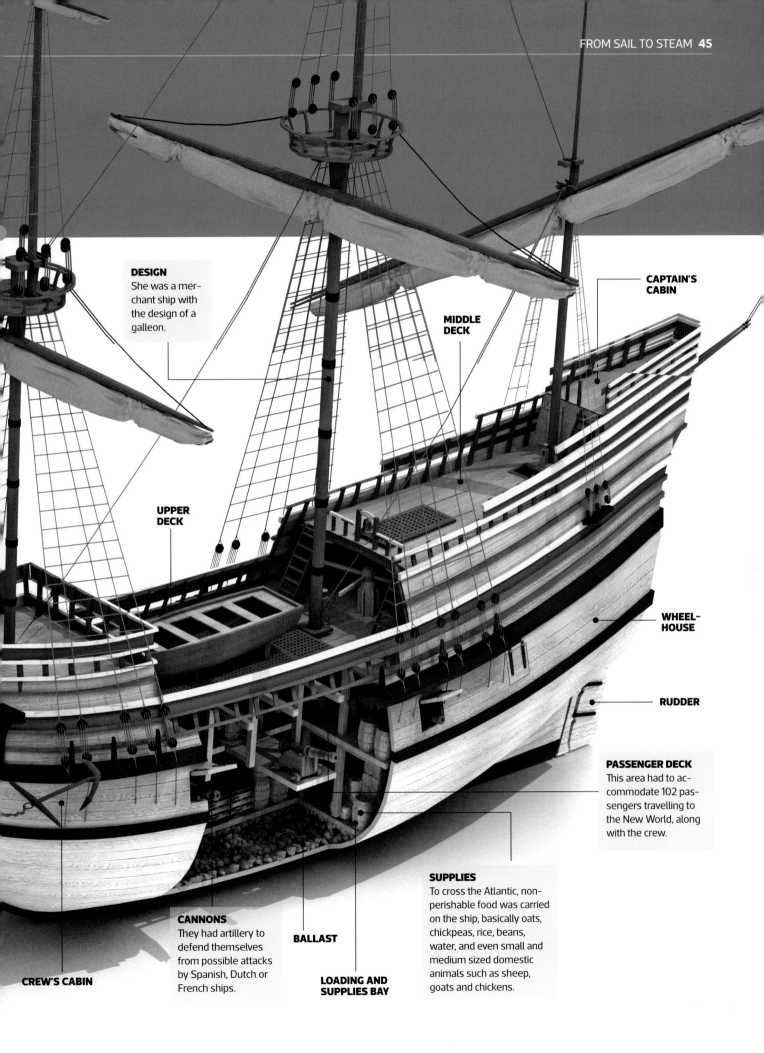

DESIGN
She was a merchant ship with the design of a galleon.

MIDDLE DECK

CAPTAIN'S CABIN

UPPER DECK

WHEEL-HOUSE

RUDDER

PASSENGER DECK
This area had to accommodate 102 passengers travelling to the New World, along with the crew.

CREW'S CABIN

CANNONS
They had artillery to defend themselves from possible attacks by Spanish, Dutch or French ships.

BALLAST

LOADING AND SUPPLIES BAY

SUPPLIES
To cross the Atlantic, non-perishable food was carried on the ship, basically oats, chickpeas, rice, beans, water, and even small and medium sized domestic animals such as sheep, goats and chickens.

Pirate ships

Between the sixteenth and eighteenth centuries, piracy hit the trade routes to the new colonies in America and Africa, mainly in the Caribbean. They had fast ships, with a lot of armament and a shallow draft for easy access to the coast.

Queen Anne's Revenge

The flagship of the legendary Blackbeard was one of the emblems of the pirate ships. Built in 1710 and stolen by the French in 1712 to be used it as a slave ship, it was finally recovered by the English, who allocated her to piracy. Commanded by Blackbeard, she struck terror into the coasts of Africa and the Caribbean.

TECHNICAL SHEET

▸ **Type:** Frigate
▸ **Crew:** Around 125 men
▸ **Dimensions:**

7.5 m
Beam

32 m
Length

SLING
Strong line that avoided the displacement of the gun in recoil.

TACKLES
Ropes that by rigging and blocks placed the gun looking inwards or on battery to fire.

GUN PLUG

BOWSPRIT

TAIL-TACKLE
Used to move the gun, it also served to hold it during navigation or when inactive.

CARRIAGE
Structure that bore the weight of the gun. It weighed about 900 kg.

CANNON BALLS

BREECH-LOADER
It was used to push the load into the gun.

ANCHOR
It weighed about 1,500 kg, and possibly required an hour's work for its lifting.

BLACKBEARD'S EMBLEM

FORE-MAST

MIZZEN

RIGGING
The ship had three masts and eight sails.

MAIN MAST

CAPTAIN'S QUARTERS
It was in one of the most stable areas of the ship in case of bad weather and the best defensive point in case of riots.

ARMAMENT
She carried about 40 guns, operated by four people each, which fired 10 kg balls.

SUPPLIES

Blackbeard

He was a sailor of the Royal Navy called Edward Teach who, after retirement, dedicated to piracy in the Caribbean Sea under the name of "Blackbeard." Legendary and feared for his exploits, he died in 1718 during a raid organized by the governor of Virginia.

The *HMS Victory*

The ships of the line, with their usual three masts and square sails, have been the best weapons in naval battles since the seventeenth century. The most emblematic of them was the ship of Admiral Nelson at Trafalgar, the *HMS Victory*.

Victorious in Trafalgar

Flagship of Admiral Horatio Nelson (1758-1805), the *HMS Victory* became historically famous after the British victory over the French-Spanish fleet at Trafalgar, the most important naval battle of the Modern Age together with that of Lepanto. This huge ship of the line had six levels, 37 sails and her main mast loomed 62.4 m above the waterline. For her construction, the wood of 6,000 oaks, elms and evergreen oaks was required.

TECHNICAL SHEET

- **Type:** Ship of the line
- **Crew:** 850 (in 1805).
- **Dimensions:**

15.7 m
Beam

69.2 m
Length

MASTS
The masts and bowsprit were divided into three sections and built with pine or spruce, for being lighter.

GALLERIES
In the aft, there were areas of leisure and rest for the captain and officers.

GUNS
At Trafalgar, the HMS *Victory* carried 104 guns spread over three decks. At the decisive moment of the battle, a cannon operated by 12 men reached one fire per minute.

SEALED
This lower deck below the water-line was used as a storage room, lounge and as an operating room in combat.

CELLAR
It could store food for six months. It also housed the ballast.

Armament

The *HMS Victory* was a three-decker. In the first deck (above the waterline) there were 30 32-pounders; on the second deck, 28 24-pounders; and on the third, 30 12-pounders. There were other 12 12-pounder guns on the quarterdeck and two more in the forecastle, which also had two carronades (short-range guns).

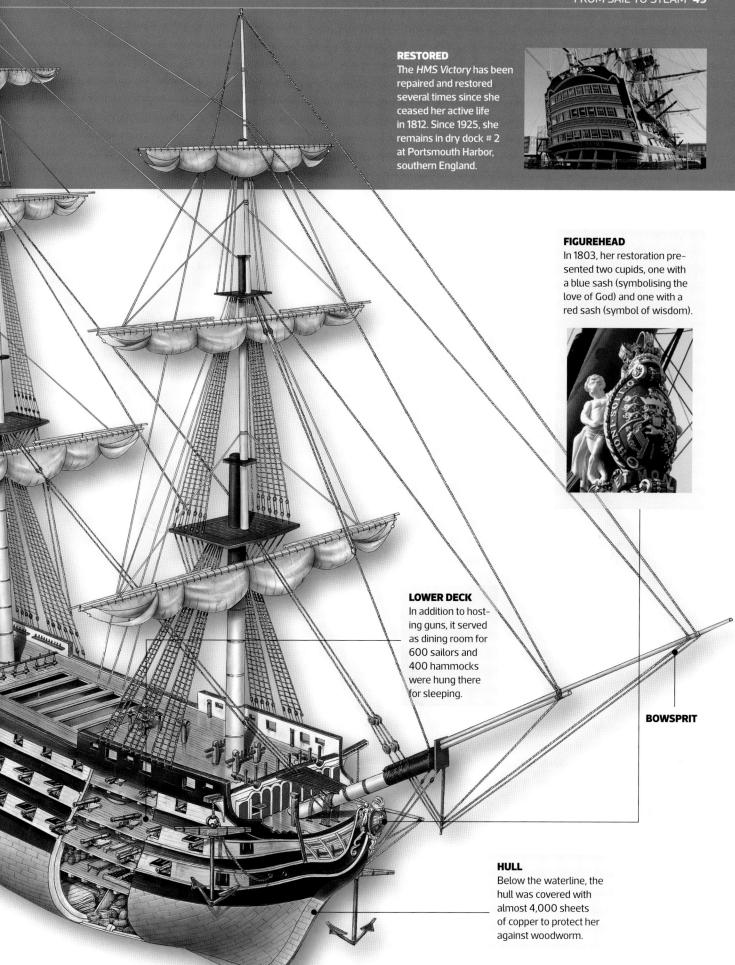

RESTORED
The *HMS Victory* has been repaired and restored several times since she ceased her active life in 1812. Since 1925, she remains in dry dock # 2 at Portsmouth Harbor, southern England.

FIGUREHEAD
In 1803, her restoration presented two cupids, one with a blue sash (symbolising the love of God) and one with a red sash (symbol of wisdom).

LOWER DECK
In addition to hosting guns, it served as dining room for 600 sailors and 400 hammocks were hung there for sleeping.

BOWSPRIT

HULL
Below the waterline, the hull was covered with almost 4,000 sheets of copper to protect her against woodworm.

The arrival of steam

Despite being dubbed as "steam coffin," the *Savannah* showed, in 1819, that it was possible for a steamship to cross the Atlantic. However, it took another 20 years until the public was prepared to rely on this type of vessel.

Helping the sail

The *Savannah* was originally built as a sailing ship. But in the end, a steam engine with two side-wheel paddles was added for her use in calm waters and when the sails could not provide a speed higher than four knots.

TECHNICAL SHEET

▶ **Type:** Hybrid three-masted sailing ship and side-wheel steamer

▶ **Dimensions:**

7.6 m
Beam

30 m
Length

RIGGING
The ship had three masts and nine square sails, plus jibs, stays and gaff rig.

FOR PASSENGERSS
She had 16 cabins with two berths in each and three saloon.

FORE-MAST

ANCHORS
They used iron chains instead of ropes, an improvement that started being used at that time.

BOWSPRIT

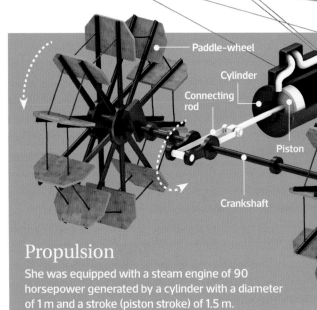

Paddle-wheel

Cylinder

Connecting rod

Piston

Crankshaft

The steam boiler pressure pushes the piston

Steam towards the outside

Propulsion

She was equipped with a steam engine of 90 horsepower generated by a cylinder with a diameter of 1 m and a stroke (piston stroke) of 1.5 m.

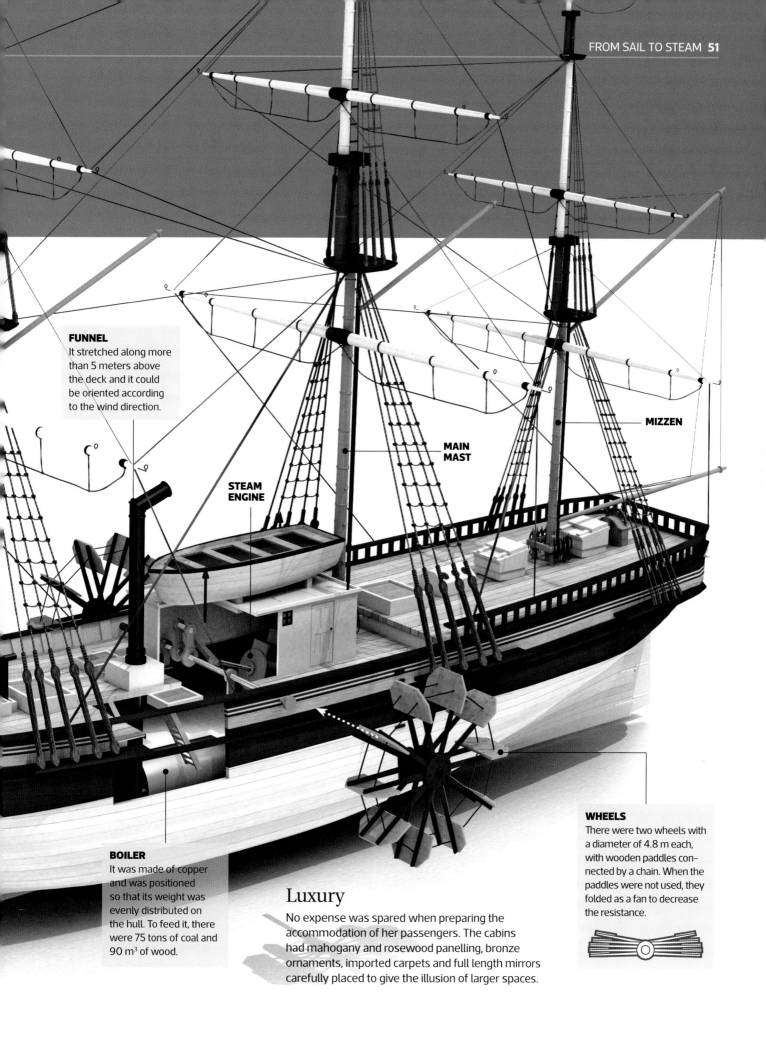

FUNNEL
It stretched along more than 5 meters above the deck and it could be oriented according to the wind direction.

MIZZEN

MAIN MAST

STEAM ENGINE

BOILER
It was made of copper and was positioned so that its weight was evenly distributed on the hull. To feed it, there were 75 tons of coal and 90 m³ of wood.

WHEELS
There were two wheels with a diameter of 4.8 m each, with wooden paddles connected by a chain. When the paddles were not used, they folded as a fan to decrease the resistance.

Luxury

No expense was spared when preparing the accommodation of her passengers. The cabins had mahogany and rosewood panelling, bronze ornaments, imported carpets and full length mirrors carefully placed to give the illusion of larger spaces.

The *HMS Beagle*

Initially built as a brig and amended as barque, this ship came to fame for taking Charles Darwin on board, the naturalist author of the theory of evolution in his study trip around the world between 1831 and 1836.

The barque

This type of craft derived from the brig appeared in the second half of the seventeenth century and was widely used until the nineteenth century. It was characterized by the large area covered by its sail set, ideal for ocean travel.

TECHNICAL SHEET

▸ **Type:** Barque
▸ **Crew:** 65 people (2nd trip)
▸ **Dimensions:**

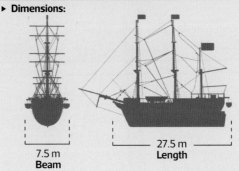

7.5 m
Beam

27.5 m
Length

DARWIN'S CABIN

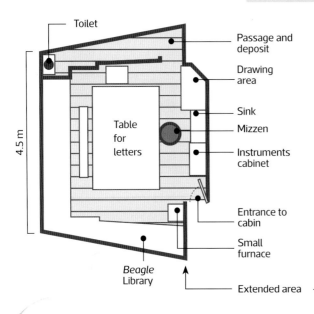

Toilet

Passage and deposit

Drawing area

Sink

Mizzen

Instruments cabinet

Table for letters

4.5 m

Entrance to cabin

Small furnace

Beagle Library

Extended area

RIGGING
She had 6 square sails in the main-mast and fore-mast, two gaff rig sails on the mizzen, and jib sails and staysails.

Charles Darwin (1809-1882)

This English naturalist formulated between 1837 and 1839 the theory of evolution by natural selection after returning from a trip around the world aboard the *HMS Beagle*, but it was not until two decades later that he finally gave it full public release in *The Origin of Species*, a book that profoundly influenced the thinking of modern Western society.

BEFORE AND AFTER

Brig of 10 guns (1820)

Barque (1825)

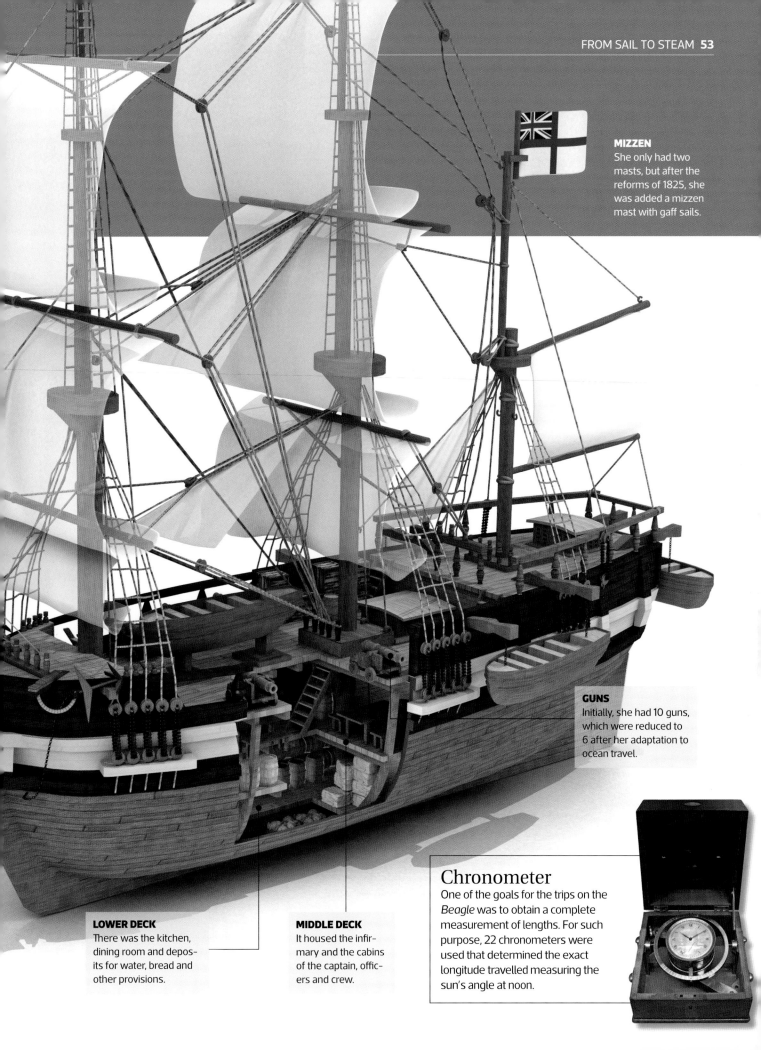

MIZZEN
She only had two masts, but after the reforms of 1825, she was added a mizzen mast with gaff sails.

GUNS
Initially, she had 10 guns, which were reduced to 6 after her adaptation to ocean travel.

Chronometer
One of the goals for the trips on the *Beagle* was to obtain a complete measurement of lengths. For such purpose, 22 chronometers were used that determined the exact longitude travelled measuring the sun's angle at noon.

LOWER DECK
There was the kitchen, dining room and deposits for water, bread and other provisions.

MIDDLE DECK
It housed the infirmary and the cabins of the captain, officers and crew.

The clippers

These extremely fast and slender ships could travel enormous distances without touching port to reload coal. The opening of the Suez Canal (1869) made them lose their advantage over steamboats.

The *Cutty Sark*

Built in Dumbarton (Scotland), she was one of the last clippers, and the fastest of all. She operated between 1869 and 1895 under the English flag dedicated to tea and wool trade, before doing it under the Portuguese flag. The elegance of her line and speed made her a legend

SAILS AND RIGGING
Her arrangement, called *tea rag*, maximized the sails to achieve the greatest possible propulsion.

CARGO HATCHES
There were two on the main deck, where there also were the crew cabins.

TECHNICAL SHEET

- ▸ **Type:** Clipper
- ▸ **Crew:** 100 men
- ▸ **Dimensions:**

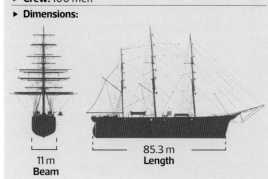

11 m
Beam

85.3 m
Length

COMPOSITE CONSTRUCTION
Unlike US clippers, made of wood, clippers such as the *Cutty Sark* combined wood and steel.

FIGUREHEAD
The ship's name comes from a poem entitled Tam O'Shanter, starring the witch Nannie whose only clothing was a very short shirt made of linen and called cutty sark. Nannie is depicted in the figurehead.

HULL
It was designed and inspired by The Tweed, a fast frigate of the time.

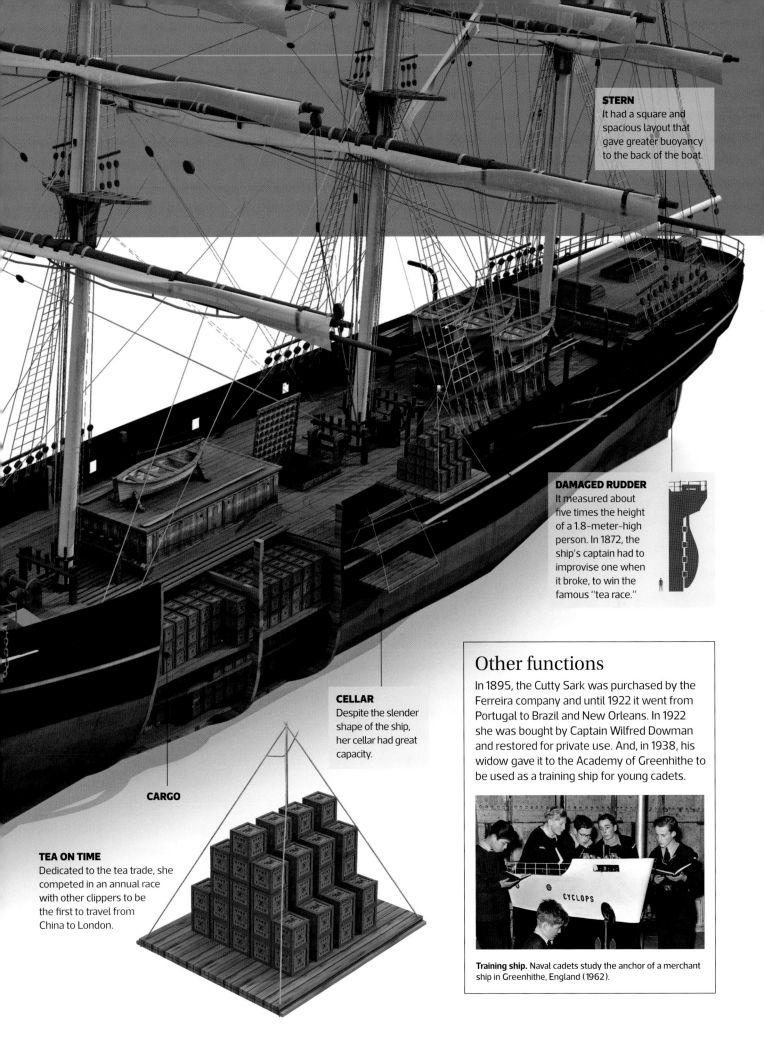

STERN
It had a square and spacious layout that gave greater buoyancy to the back of the boat.

DAMAGED RUDDER
It measured about five times the height of a 1.8-meter-high person. In 1872, the ship's captain had to improvise one when it broke, to win the famous "tea race."

CELLAR
Despite the slender shape of the ship, her cellar had great capacity.

CARGO

TEA ON TIME
Dedicated to the tea trade, she competed in an annual race with other clippers to be the first to travel from China to London.

Other functions

In 1895, the Cutty Sark was purchased by the Ferreira company and until 1922 it went from Portugal to Brazil and New Orleans. In 1922 she was bought by Captain Wilfred Dowman and restored for private use. And, in 1938, his widow gave it to the Academy of Greenhithe to be used as a training ship for young cadets.

Training ship. Naval cadets study the anchor of a merchant ship in Greenhithe, England (1962).

The first battleships

In the late nineteenth century, large warships began to be built without sails and they were called battleships, which were characterized by strong steel armor and for incorporating large artillery pieces mounted on turrets, plus lightweight batteries.

The Japanese *Mikasa*

This battleship was one of the best of her era and the result of the naval expansion program initiated by Japan in 1896 that lasted 10 years. Thus, the Japanese commissioned the construction of their war fleet to Great Britain, France and Italy, based on battleships. The *Mikasa* was the sixth ship built in England and became the flagship of Japanese naval hero and admiral Tōgō Heihachirō during the 1904–1905 Russo-Japanese War.

TECHNICAL SHEET

▸ **Type:** Battleship
▸ **Crew:** 850 men
▸ **Dimensions:**

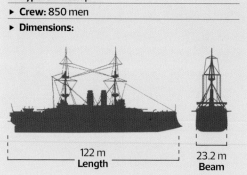

122 m
Length

23.2 m
Beam

BRIDGE
Focal point of the battleship, it was the place where the officers met to make decisions.

ARTILLERY
In addition to the main guns, the *Mikasa* had other 46 guns available to increase firepower: 14 of 154 mm, 20 of 76 mm, 8 of 47 mm and 4 of 35 mm.

MAIN GUNS
She was equipped with two double steel guns, one aft and one on the bow, which were able to shoot three 305 mm shells every two minutes, with a range of 10 km. The forward turret had 40 men assigned.

EMBLEM
The bow sported the Japanese imperial emblem, a golden chrysanthemum flower.

JAPANESE EMBLEM
After exploding due to a short circuit, the *Mikasa* was refloated and rebuilt in 1922 as a national monument in the military port of Yokosuka (Japan).

LIFEBOATS
They were strategically placed in case a torpedo opened a waterways and the sinking was slow. Salvage was useless if the explosion occurred in the powder deposit or boilers.

TELEGRAPH CABIN
Incorporated into the Navy in the early twentieth century, wireless telegraphy was decisive for the development of Japanese tactics in the Battle of Tsushima.

PROPULSION
The steam gave an advantage to battleships over sailing ships in the Crimean War (1854-1855). Smoke and steam were expelled by large combustion funnels.

STORAGE
Carbon deposits accumulated fuel for 25 boilers and two engines.

ARMORED
The steel shield protected the hull and especially the bridge.

The ironclad

They were the first actual battleships, i.e., the first steam warships armored with iron or steel plates that replaced the wooden vessels, which very vulnerable to explosive shells. The French Navy was the first to build an ironclad, the *La Gloire* ship (1859). The British answered a year later with the manufacture of *HMS Warrior*.

La Gloire. Illustration of the French warship, the first ironclad in history.

The *RRS Discovery*

In the late nineteenth and early twentieth century there was a peak of expeditions to unexplored places on earth. The *RRS Discovery* was specifically built with one goal: to explore Antarctica.

Last of its kind

The *Discovery* was built in Dundee, Scotland, by Dundee Shipbuilders Company and she was the last wooden ship with three masts manufactured in the UK. The construction of the *Discovery* only required five days, between March 16 and 21, 1901, when it was launched.

TECHNICAL SHEET

▸ **Type:** three-masted sailboat
▸ **Crew:** 11 officers and 36 crew members
▸ **Dimensions:**

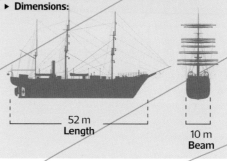

52 m
Length

10 m
Beam

BOW
To avoid interfering in magnetic research, the metal parts were made of bronze.

DISCOVERY

Trapped in the ice

The expedition, led by Captain Robert Scott and the explorer Ernest Shackleton, spent two years in the white continent since the Discovery was trapped in the ice and had to wait to be rescued.

The ships sent for the rescue used explosives to release her.

HULL
It was made of five different types of wood so that the ship could withstand the pressure of the ice.

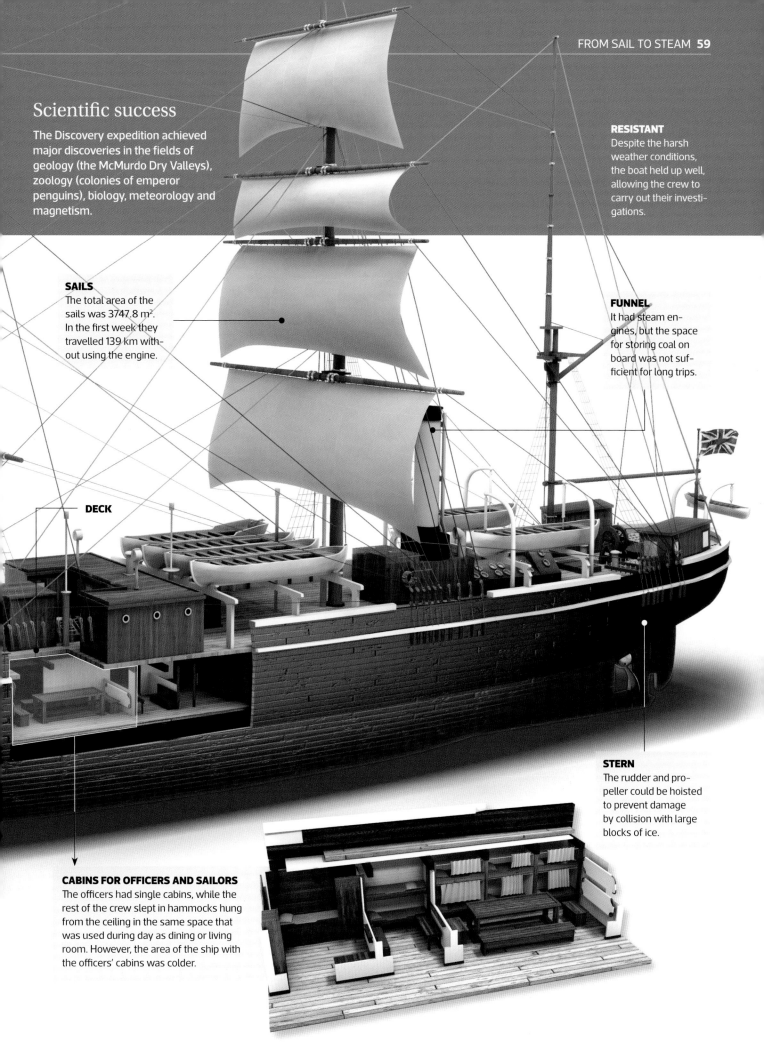

Scientific success

The Discovery expedition achieved major discoveries in the fields of geology (the McMurdo Dry Valleys), zoology (colonies of emperor penguins), biology, meteorology and magnetism.

RESISTANT
Despite the harsh weather conditions, the boat held up well, allowing the crew to carry out their investigations.

SAILS
The total area of the sails was 3747.8 m². In the first week they travelled 139 km without using the engine.

FUNNEL
It had steam engines, but the space for storing coal on board was not sufficient for long trips.

DECK

STERN
The rudder and propeller could be hoisted to prevent damage by collision with large blocks of ice.

CABINS FOR OFFICERS AND SAILORS
The officers had single cabins, while the rest of the crew slept in hammocks hung from the ceiling in the same space that was used during day as dining or living room. However, the area of the ship with the officers' cabins was colder.

The last great sailing ships

Until the opening of the Panama Canal in 1914, Cape Horn was one of the key maritime trade routes. To overcome its harsh sailing conditions, European shipping companies built huge sailboats of great tonnage and up to six masts.

The *Cape Horners*

The "gold rush" in California led to a race between European companies to reach the wealth and raw materials of the American Pacific coast, which resulted in the late nineteenth century in the manufacture of portentous sailboats, known as *Cape Horners* since they had to round the complicated Cape Horn. Many, like the Potosi the Preussen, belonged to the fleet of the Hamburg shipping company Laeisz, the most important one of that time.

SAILS
Some of these sailboats had over 6,000 m² of sail surface, which allowed them to reach speeds of over 15 knots.

BOOM

GAFF SAIL-BOOM

BONAVENTURE MIZZEN

MIZZEN

MAINROYAL TOP

TOPGALLANT SAIL

MAST-TOP

TOPMAST

STERN MAINMAST

TOP

LOWER MAST

The "P-Line"

Since 1880, all merchant sailing ships of the German shipping company Laeisz were assigned a name that began with P: Pampa, Pamir, Passat, Priwall, Preussen... (image)–. Hence it became known as the "P-Line."

CELLARS
They exceeded the 6,000-ton capacity. The Freussen could carry up to 60 thousand bags of salt.

DISTINCTIVE
All the Laeisz merchants had a green stripe on the waterline and red below.

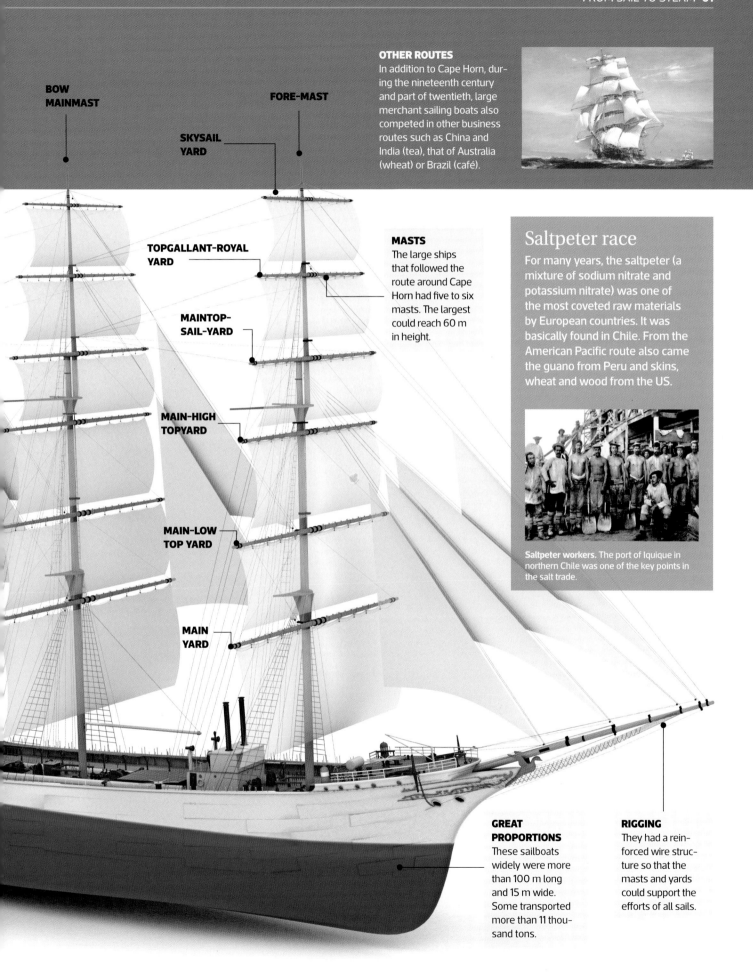

**BOW
MAINMAST**

FORE-MAST

**SKYSAIL
YARD**

**TOPGALLANT-ROYAL
YARD**

**MAINTOP-
SAIL-YARD**

**MAIN-HIGH
TOPYARD**

**MAIN-LOW
TOP YARD**

**MAIN
YARD**

OTHER ROUTES
In addition to Cape Horn, during the nineteenth century and part of twentieth, large merchant sailing boats also competed in other business routes such as China and India (tea), that of Australia (wheat) or Brazil (café).

MASTS
The large ships that followed the route around Cape Horn had five to six masts. The largest could reach 60 m in height.

Saltpeter race

For many years, the saltpeter (a mixture of sodium nitrate and potassium nitrate) was one of the most coveted raw materials by European countries. It was basically found in Chile. From the American Pacific route also came the guano from Peru and skins, wheat and wood from the US.

Saltpeter workers. The port of Iquique in northern Chile was one of the key points in the salt trade.

**GREAT
PROPORTIONS**
These sailboats widely were more than 100 m long and 15 m wide. Some transported more than 11 thousand tons.

RIGGING
They had a reinforced wire structure so that the masts and yards could support the efforts of all sails.

Naval engineers

During the nineteenth century and part of the twentieth, naval engineering evolved significantly and increasingly bigger, safer and faster ships were built to meet the needs of the merchant and war fleets of maritime powers.

Great advances

In the context of the Industrial Revolution and the emergence of large shipping companies competing for hegemony of the new transoceanic routes, naval engineering experienced a decisive boost. First with the application of steam and iron, then with the use of the propeller and the introduction of steel to create stronger and lighter hulls, and later with the use of new propulsion systems. Thus, ships increased their size and performance in terms of speed, stability and comfort.

FIRST TEST
This is a scale replica of the first steamship Fulton tested on the Seine, Paris, in 1803.

Steam propulsion

In 1807, the *Clermont* made her first trip up the Hudson River in the United States. Devised by engineer Robert Fulton, she was the first steamboat, propelled by side paddles, to be commercially successful. From that time, the steamships multiplied.

Referents of marine engineering

The great engineers of the time were English, but also the French and North American made significant contributions.

ROBERT FULTON
After many attempts, this US engineer was the first to successfully apply Watt's steam engine in a vessel, the *Clermont*.

FRANCIS PETTIT SMITH
English inventor who developed propulsion by helices solving the handicap of boring holes below the waterline. In 1939, he gave a demonstration in his *SS Archimedes*.

W. F. Gibbs and ships of the line

William Francis Gibbs, from the US, was one of the great naval engineers of the first half of the twentieth century. He built over 6,000 ships of the line, most notably the *SS America* (1940) –picture– and especially the *SS United States* States (1952), which during its maiden voyage crossed the Atlantic in just three days and ten hours, at an average speed of 35 knots.

DUPUY DE LOME
This French naval architect pioneered the construction of ironclad warships propelled by steam. The *Gloire* (1858) was the first one.

First submarines

During the nineteenth century, the Spanish Narcís Monturiol and Isaac Peral achieved decisive breakthroughs in the field of underwater navigation although they had little support. Monturiol made the first manned submarine with an anaerobic propulsion system [*Ictineo II* (1854)] while Peral invented in 1888 the first submarine capable of launching torpedoes.

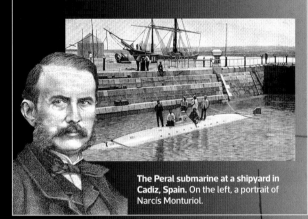

The Peral submarine at a shipyard in Cadiz, Spain. On the left, a portrait of Narcís Monturiol.

A TRANSATLANTIC GIANT
Conceived by Isambard K. Brunel, the SS *Great Eastern* (1858) was the largest ocean liner built in the nineteenth century. It was 212 m long and had a capacity of 4,000 passengers, who enjoyed every kind of luxury. To the right, the ship in Blackwall (England) during construction.

ROBERT SEPPINGS
This English naval architect invented a system to elevate the ships in dry dock that significantly reduced the time and labor on repairs.

ISAMBARD K. BRUNEL
He was one of the great engineers of the nineteenth cen- tury, also in the field of railways. He built the first iron-hulled liner, the *Great Western* (1838).

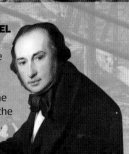

THOMAS ANDREWS
English engineer responsible for the construction of the *Titanic*, on which he was travelling when it sank, and other great liners of the White Star Line.

Contemporary navigation

Chapter 3

In the first decades of the twentieth century, the great ocean liners lived their golden age. They plied the oceans carrying thousands of passengers without skimping on comfort and luxury, although there also were tragic endings. The sinking of the *Titanic* (1911) is probably the most famous of them. It was also the golden age of paddle-wheel steamboats, which performed regular river transport services. The sight of these vessels plying the Mississippi is an icon of the era. Military vessels also experienced great development. Great battleships such as the *Dreadnought* began a race among the major powers of the time to provide themselves with the best warships. During the following decades, submarines and aircraft carriers became key parts for naval warfare. Technological advances also allowed a shift in ocean exploration, as demonstrated by Jacques Cousteau aboard the *Calypso*. In a very different way, multiple explorers tried to emulate our ancestors with vessels similar to those used in the past to show that thousands of years ago they were already able to navigate the oceans performing amazing feats. Today, there are container ships capable of carrying thousands of tons of goods in one trip, and huge floating hotels offer luxury cruises around the world.

HMS Dreadnought

In 1906, the *HMS Dreadnought* of the British Royal Navy marked a giant leap in military naval technology, and made all the battleships of her kind that followed receive the generic name of dreadnought.

High tech

Given her new system of steam turbines, she was the fastest ship in the world. In addition, she counted with a uniform battery of cannons as they were all of the same caliber.

TECHNICAL SHEET

▸ **Type:** Battleship

▸ **Crew:** Up to 773

▸ **Dimensions:**

25 m
Beam

160.6 m
Length

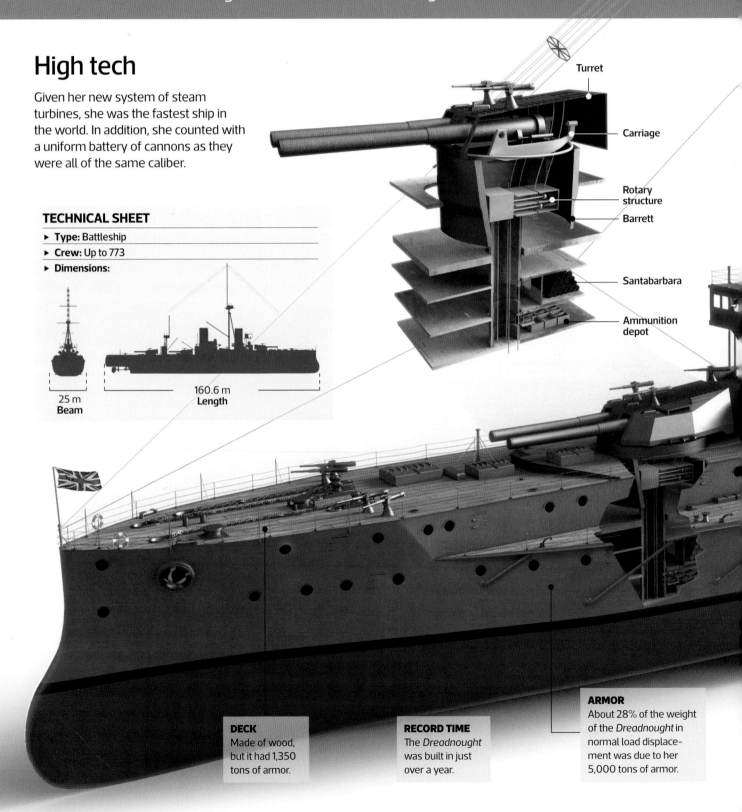

Turret

Carriage

Rotary structure

Barrett

Santabarbara

Ammunition depot

DECK
Made of wood, but it had 1,350 tons of armor.

RECORD TIME
The *Dreadnought* was built in just over a year.

ARMOR
About 28% of the weight of the *Dreadnought* in normal load displacement was due to her 5,000 tons of armor.

A peculiar victory

The *Dreadnought* never got into battle because she was being repaired when she could have, within the context of the Battle of Jutland (1916). However, on March 18, 1915, she sank a German submarine (the *U–29*) not by gunfire, by ramming.

RANGEFINDERS
They were used to measure distances and set the fire-control.

MANEUVERABILITY
It was ensured by two parallel offset rudders, acting behind the propellers and four axle lines.

DEFENCES
She counted with smaller batteries of cannons and torpedo tubes.

FUNNEL

Steam turbine

The ship had four Parsons steam turbines, the most modern of their time.

Steam inlet

Fixed blades

Rotating blades

Steam output at low pressure

BATTERIES
She had five batteries, each armed with two 305 mm cannons. Its great fire-power allowed her to maintain combat at a long range.

DOUBLE DIRECTION
It could fire eight of her ten powerful cannons at the same time towards opposite directions.

RMS *Titanic*

This liner was the largest ship in the world at her time. She sank on her maiden voyage in the early hours of April 15, 1912, after colliding with an iceberg. 1514 of the 2223 people aboard died.

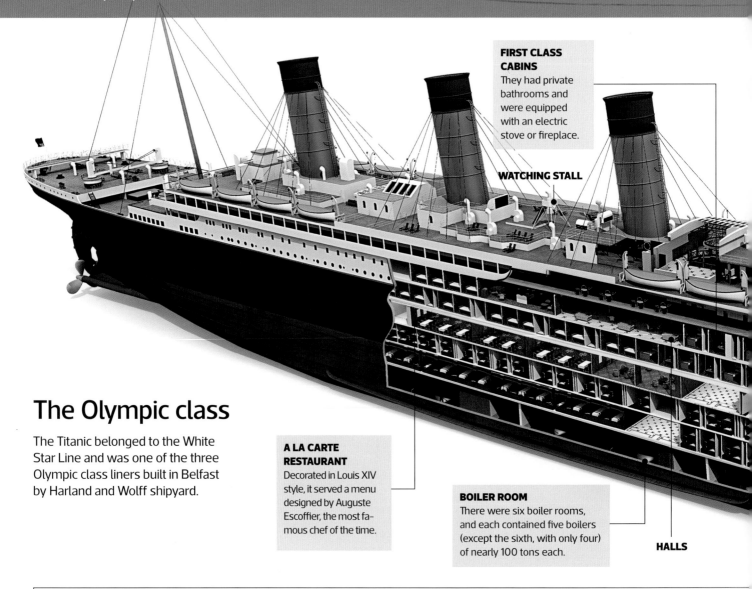

FIRST CLASS CABINS
They had private bathrooms and were equipped with an electric stove or fireplace.

WATCHING STALL

The Olympic class

The Titanic belonged to the White Star Line and was one of the three Olympic class liners built in Belfast by Harland and Wolff shipyard.

A LA CARTE RESTAURANT
Decorated in Louis XIV style, it served a menu designed by Auguste Escoffier, the most famous chef of the time.

BOILER ROOM
There were six boiler rooms, and each contained five boilers (except the sixth, with only four) of nearly 100 tons each.

HALLS

Where the accident occurred

The Titanic sank at around 600 km south of Newfoundland. Captain Smith gave the order to change course slightly to the south to avoid the icebergs area.

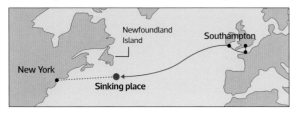

Newfoundland Island

Southampton

New York

Sinking place

The collision

Just 37 seconds after having sighted the iceberg, and after trying to avoid it, the Titanic brushed against it at a speed of 22.5 knots (41.7 km/h).

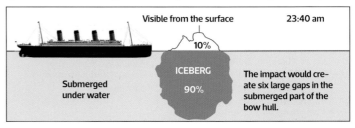

Visible from the surface   23:40 am

10%

ICEBERG

Submerged under water   90%

The impact would create six large gaps in the submerged part of the bow hull.

Grand Staircase

Symbol of luxury of the *Titanic*, there were actually two large twin staircases, one fore and one aft, exquisitely decorated, which functioned as the boarding entry for first class. The first and main stair led down to the F Deck.

PURE LUXURY
The first class decks had luxurious cabins, gyms, steam rooms, cafés, a la carte restaurants, librar-ies and a squash court.

LIFEBOATS
The ship had 20 boats, located in the upper deck: 12 fore and aft 8, capable of carrying a total of 1,178 persons.

BRIDGE

TECHNICAL SHEET

▸ **Type:** Liner
▸ **Crew:** 860
▸ **Dimensions:**

267 m
Length

28 m
Beam

TECHNOLOGICAL INNOVATIONS
The *Titanic* had four lifts, three for the first class and one for the second.

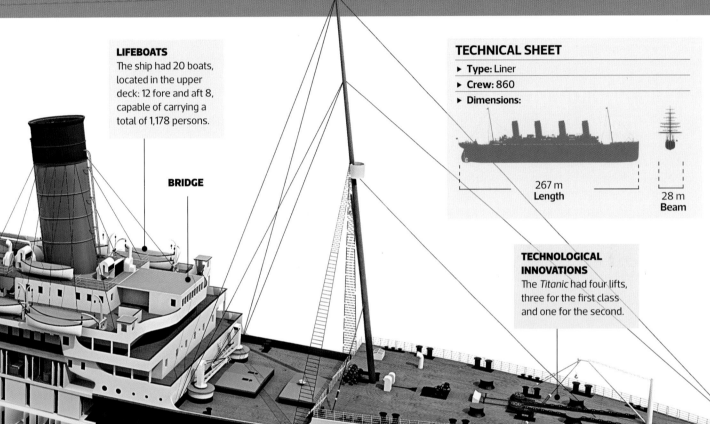

SWIMMING POOL

The sinking

The friction of the hull with the iceberg produced six gaps under the waterline that flooded five watertight compartments. If only they had been four, the boat would not have sunk.

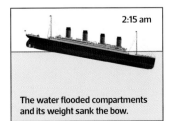

2:15 am

The water flooded compartments and its weight sank the bow.

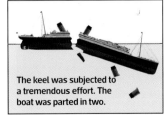

The keel was subjected to a tremendous effort. The boat was parted in two.

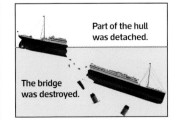

Part of the hull was detached.

The bridge was destroyed.

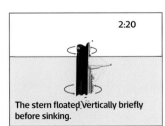

2:20

The stern floated vertically briefly before sinking.

Major shipwrecks

The great liners lived a golden age in the early twentieth century. But their history is also marked by tragedy. Other boats followed the same fate as the *Titanic*: some by accident and others due to war actions.

The sinking of the *Lusitania*

The *Lusitania* was launched in 1911 and she was one of the most luxurious passenger ships of the time. She sank on May 7, 1915, off the coast of Ireland being struck by German torpedoes. With Europe fully involved in World War II, she carried goods and passengers from New York to Liverpool, but the Germans affirmed that she also had weapons on board. 1198 people died, including 291 women and 94 children.

SURVIVORS
Out of the approximately 1900 people who were on board at the time of the wreck, only 700 survived.

Chronology of famous shipwrecks

1 **1916– *Príncipe de Asturias***
This Spanish ocean liner for cargo wrecked for striking a submerged reef off the coast of Brazil. Out of 588 passengers, 143 survived.

2 **1945– *Wilhelm Gustloff***
The German liner was torpedoed by a Soviet submarine. It carried over 10,000 refugees who fled upon the Soviet advance. 9,343 of them died.

3 **1956– *Andrea Doria***
Italian liner that performed the Genoa-New York route. It sank off the coast of Massachusetts upon crashing into another boat, the *Stockholm*. There were 51 victims, 46 of the *Andrea Doria*.

Consequences

The sinking of the *Lusitania* caused a stir in public opinion in the United States, since more than a hundred victims were from such country. The event triggered a reaction favorable to US intervention in the war, which became effective two years later.

PROPAGANDA
Poster calling for enlistment issued by the Committee on Public Safety of Boston, with an image allusive to the sinking of the *Lusitania*.

ENLIST

EXPLOSIONS
By 2 PM the *Lusitania* was hit by a torpedo fired from a German submarine. There was a second torpedo and a third detonation, the origin of which is uncertain. It only took her 18 minutes to sink.

4 **2000- *Kursk***
The nuclear Russian submarine sank in the Barents Sea, while it carried out military manoeuvres, allegedly due to a defective torpedo. The 118 crew members perished.

5 **2002- *Prestige***
The oil tanker under the flag of the Bahamas sank 250 km off the Spanish Atlantic coast, due to bad weather conditions. There were no human casualties but it meant an ecological disaster.

6 **2012- *Costa Concordia***
The Italian cruise ship sank off the Island of Giglio, after being stranded. Despite the proximity of the coast, thirty people died and over 4,200 were evacuated.

Delta Queen

Appearing in the nineteenth century, the sternwheel steamboats were very successful in river navigation, as those cruising US rivers like the Mississippi or Missouri. The *Delta Queen*, launched in 1927, was one of the most famous in its class.

Regular services

In 1807, the *Clermont* steamboat of Robert Fulton sailed the Hudson River crossing the 240 km between New York and Albany. She was the first one that established a regular steam transportation service for passengers in US rivers. The *Delta Queen* was commissioned in 1927 to operate in the Sacramento River in California and then in the western rivers of the United States. Today she is a National Monument.

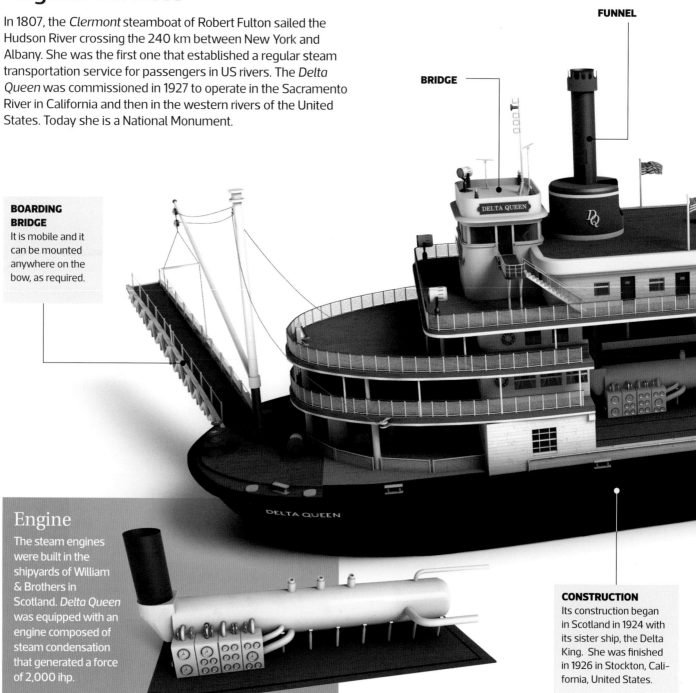

FUNNEL

BRIDGE

BOARDING BRIDGE
It is mobile and it can be mounted anywhere on the bow, as required.

Engine
The steam engines were built in the shipyards of William & Brothers in Scotland. *Delta Queen* was equipped with an engine composed of steam condensation that generated a force of 2,000 ihp.

CONSTRUCTION
Its construction began in Scotland in 1924 with its sister ship, the Delta King. She was finished in 1926 in Stockton, California, United States.

Eighty years of history

The *Delta Queen*, along with her sister ship *Delta King*, operated for the California Transportation Company of San Francisco. During WWII, the US Navy asked for her to transport troops and to attend medical emergencies. After the war, she continued serving as a river ship for passengers for different companies. She performed its last trip in 2008.

FLOATING HOTEL
Docked in Chattanooga, Tennessee, *Delta Queen* is now a floating hotel, one of the most expensive in the world.

TECHNICAL SHEET
▸ **Type:** Steam Wheel
▸ **Crew:** No data
▸ **Dimensions:** 87 m of length, 18 m of beam

A special case

The 1966 Safety at Sea Law prohibited boats mainly made of wood to carry more than 50 passengers, but, thanks to the efforts of a relevant number of congressmen, the Delta Queen was exempted from the law from 1970 to 2008.

CABINS
With capacity for 176 passengers, the Delta Queen was distinguished by its luxury.

STRUCTURE
With a weight of 1650 tons, she has a double steel hull and a superstructure of wood.

Paddlewheel

The steam engine moves a paddle wheel mounted on the stern that drove the boat through the water. The wheel is made of steel with four rows of paddles.

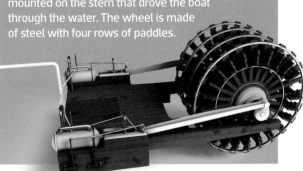

The *Bismarck*

The *Bismark* was the first of two Bismarck-class battleships launched by Nazi Navy shortly before World War II. While her operational life was brief, her armor and armament made her the most powerful battleship at that time.

TECHNICAL SHEET

▸ **Type:** Battleship
▸ **Crew:** 2,065 (plus 2,200 during Operation Rheinübung)
▸ **Dimensions:**

251 m
Length

36 m
Beam

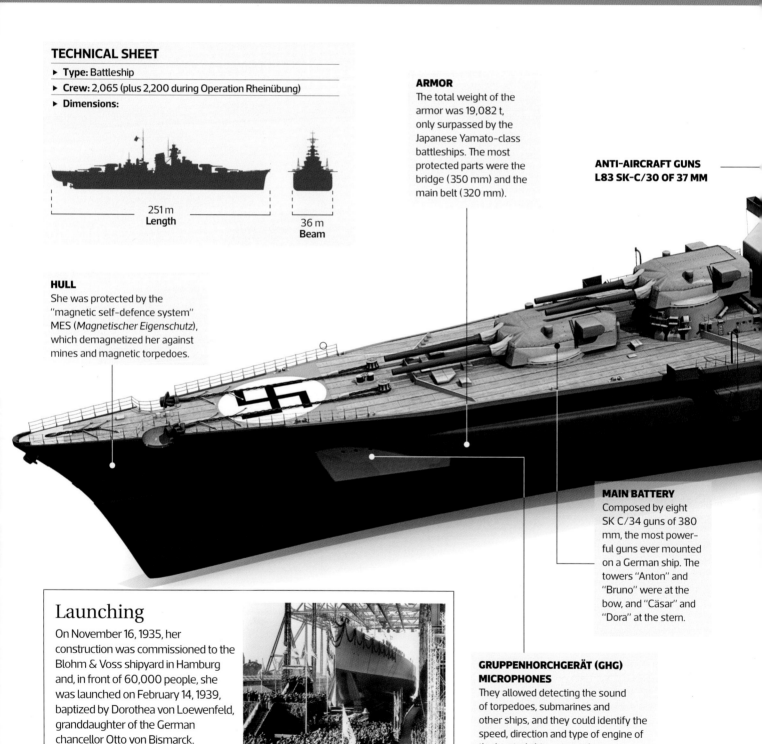

ARMOR
The total weight of the armor was 19,082 t, only surpassed by the Japanese Yamato-class battleships. The most protected parts were the bridge (350 mm) and the main belt (320 mm).

ANTI-AIRCRAFT GUNS L83 SK-C/30 OF 37 MM

HULL
She was protected by the "magnetic self-defence system" MES (*Magnetischer Eigenschutz*), which demagnetized her against mines and magnetic torpedoes.

MAIN BATTERY
Composed by eight SK C/34 guns of 380 mm, the most power-ful guns ever mounted on a German ship. The towers "Anton" and "Bruno" were at the bow, and "Cäsar" and "Dora" at the stern.

Launching

On November 16, 1935, her construction was commissioned to the Blohm & Voss shipyard in Hamburg and, in front of 60,000 people, she was launched on February 14, 1939, baptized by Dorothea von Loewenfeld, granddaughter of the German chancellor Otto von Bismarck.

GRUPPENHORCHGERÄT (GHG) MICROPHONES
They allowed detecting the sound of torpedoes, submarines and other ships, and they could identify the speed, direction and type of engine of the located ship or torpedo.

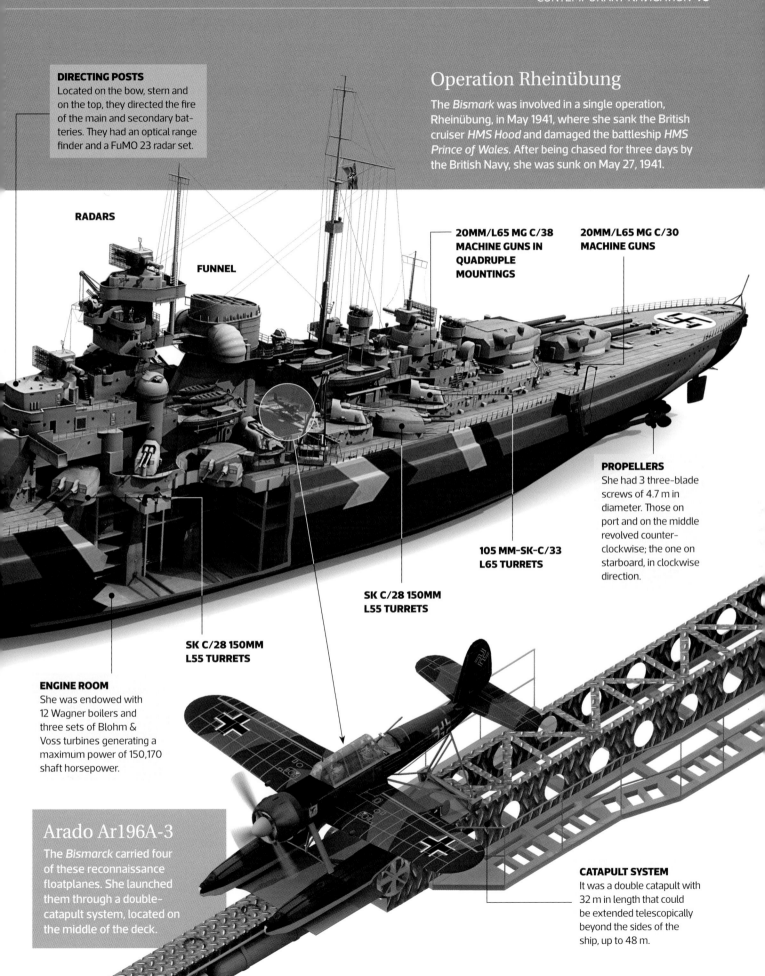

DIRECTING POSTS
Located on the bow, stern and on the top, they directed the fire of the main and secondary batteries. They had an optical range finder and a FuMO 23 radar set.

Operation Rheinübung

The *Bismark* was involved in a single operation, Rheinübung, in May 1941, where she sank the British cruiser *HMS Hood* and damaged the battleship *HMS Prince of Wales*. After being chased for three days by the British Navy, she was sunk on May 27, 1941.

RADARS

FUNNEL

20MM/L65 MG C/38 MACHINE GUNS IN QUADRUPLE MOUNTINGS

20MM/L65 MG C/30 MACHINE GUNS

PROPELLERS
She had 3 three-blade screws of 4.7 m in diameter. Those on port and on the middle revolved counter-clockwise; the one on starboard, in clockwise direction.

105 MM-SK-C/33 L65 TURRETS

SK C/28 150MM L55 TURRETS

SK C/28 150MM L55 TURRETS

ENGINE ROOM
She was endowed with 12 Wagner boilers and three sets of Blohm & Voss turbines generating a maximum power of 150,170 shaft horsepower.

Arado Ar196A-3

The *Bismarck* carried four of these reconnaissance floatplanes. She launched them through a double-catapult system, located on the middle of the deck.

CATAPULT SYSTEM
It was a double catapult with 32 m in length that could be extended telescopically beyond the sides of the ship, up to 48 m.

The *Kon-Tiki*

In 1947, the Norwegian explorer Thor Heyerdahl performed an expedition across the Pacific Ocean from Peru to Polynesia travelling 7,000 miles aboard the Kon-Tiki, a raft that emulated those used by pre-Columbian peoples.

The expedition

Heyerdahl argued that Polynesia had been colonized by ancient pre-Columbian peoples. To prove his theories, he built a raft with tree trunks and natural materials in the style of ancient native boats from Peru following the descriptions of texts by Spanish conquistadors. After 101 days of sailing, with this boat and a crew of six men, he successfully performed the expedition that the pre-Inca peoples allegedly did over a thousand years ago.

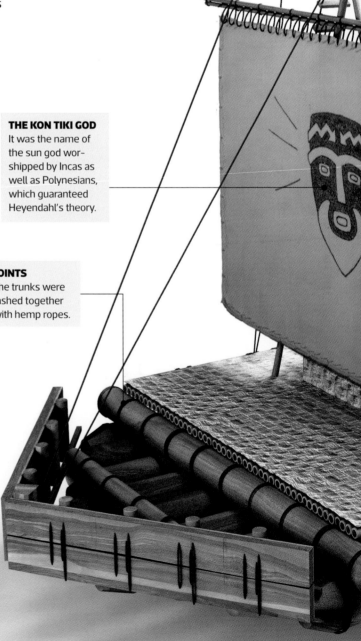

MAST
It was 9 meters high.

THE KON TIKI GOD
It was the name of the sun god worshipped by Incas as well as Polynesians, which guaranteed Heyendahl's theory.

JOINTS
The trunks were lashed together with hemp ropes.

The load

The expedition left with some food and it had some modern elements like a radio and a sextant.

WATER
The expedition departed with 1,000 liters of drinking water.

FOOD
They carried 200 pieces on board including coconuts, potatoes, pumpkins and other fruits and roots.

OTHER SUPPLIES
During the trip they supplied themselves from sea goods: they fished from tuna to sharks.

OTHER ELEMENTS
They had a NC-173 radio receiver, as well as watches, maps, a sextant and steel knives.

The ideologue

Thor Heyendahl (1914-2002), Norwegian explorer and biologist. He devoted much of his career to study the migration of primitive peoples. Thus, he performed other expeditions similar to that of *Kon-Tiki*, i.e. one from Egypt to America on a raft made of papyrus, or one through the Indian Ocean with a reed boat.

SALE SUCCESS
The feat of the *Kon-Tiki* was reported by Heyendahl in a book and it was also taken to film theaters in a documentary that won an Oscar in 1951.

TECHNICAL SHEET
- **Type:** Trunk raft
- **Crew:** 6
- **Dimensions:** 15 m of length and 5 m of beam

SAIL
It had a square sail of 27 m². It was fixed, which did not give room for maneuvering.

STRUCTURE
The raft was built with 18 crossed wooden trunks. The nine trunks of the main body were 13.7 meters long and had 60 cm in diameter.

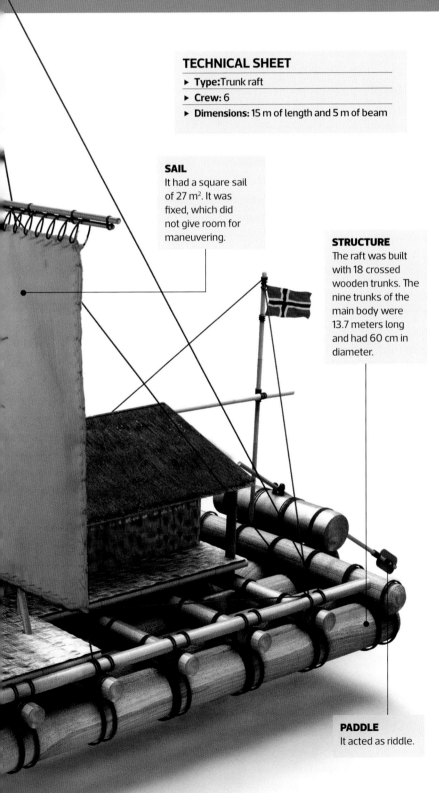

PADDLE
It acted as riddle.

Other expeditions

Many scientists and adventurers have tried to prove their theories on navigation capability and migrations of ancient civilizations. Here are some examples.

FOU PO
Frenchman Eric De Bisschop explored the south-western Pacific Ocean aboard a Chinese junk between 1932 and 1935.

SEVEN LITTLE SISTERS
In 1954, William Willis performed a trip from Peru to Samoa with a wooden raft in 155 days.

THE BALSAS (RAFTS)
The Spanish Vital Alsar conducted in 1973 the longest expedition (14,000 km) from Ecuador to Australia with three wooden rafts.

MATA RANGI III
With this boat of reeds, the Spanish Kitín Muñoz attempted to cross the Atlantic in 2001, but failed to meet the target.

Great sailing voyages

The desire to navigate the seas of the world, reached its peak as from the 19th century when fearless sailors decided to sail for adventure. The most well-known men dating from that time was Joshua Slocum, who traveled for years over 74,000 km around the world.

Greatest achievements

After Joshua Scolum, many other well-known men appeared. Alain Gerbault, Vito Dumas, Robin Knox-Johnston, Chay Blith... There are many renowned names in the list of approximately 200 sailors that travelled around the world alone. Characters that were worthy of Poseidon care driven by the wind and by an exploring and adventurous spirit.

JOSHUA SLOCUM - 1895
Ship: Spray (sailboat).
Departure harbor: Boston
Voyage: This pioneer, who succeeded in becoming the first man who travelled around the world alone, departed on the 24th of April 2895 and travelled for a total of 46,000 miles in 3 years, 2 months and 2 days.

28/2/1969
Bernard Moitessier abandoned Golden Globe Race and went on to the East by arriving at Thaiti.

ATLANTIC OCEAN

Boston

NORTH AMERICA

ATLANTIC OCEAN

CARIBBEAN SEA

Haiti

PACIFIC OCEAN

SOUTH AMERICA

Buenos Aires

Cape Horn

Back to the beginning

Because of the 50th anniversary of the first Golden Globe Race, in 2018 a special edition will be played with boats designed before 1988 without satellites or autopilots. The image shows Knox-Johnston, the first winner.

ASIA

EUROPE

3 **Francis Chichester – 1966**
Ship: Gipsy Moth IV. *Departure harbor:* Plymouth. *Voyage:* it sailed on the 27th of August and returned after 226 days. It sailed a total of 47,000 kilometers alone with only one stop in Sydney, Australia.

4 **Robin Knox-Johnston – 1968**
Ship: Suhaili. *Departure harbor:* Falmouth. *Voyage:* as a sailor of the Golden Globe Race, he departed from the harbor on the 14th of June 1968 and came back on the 22nd of April 1969, being then officially declared as the first man ever to have circumnavigating the globe non-stop.

5 **Bernard Moitessier – 1968**
Ship: Joshua. *Departure harbor:* Plymouth. *Voyage:* also a sailor of the Golden Globe Race, he started its long trip around the world on the 22nd of August 1968. Even though he abandoned the competence, he crossed the planet in a journey of 37,455 nautical miles which meant ten months of navigation– He returned on the 19th of June 1969.

PACIFIC OCEAN

6 **Chay Blith – 1970**
Ship: British Steel. *Departure harbor:* Southampton. *Voyage:* he achieved the goal of travelling around the world non-stop by the "impossible route," that is on the opposite way of "the wrong way," against important winds and currents. He departed on the 18th of October 1970 and finished the route on the 6th of August 1971, in a total of 292 days. As a result, he was named Commander of the British Empire.

AFRICA

2 **VITO DUMAS - 1942**
Ship: Lehg II. *Departure harbor:* Buenos Aires. *Voyage:* He left on the 27th of June and came back on the 7th of September 1943. In total, they were 437 days, 274 out of which, he spent sailing. He travelled for 20,420 nautical miles (37,818 km) along three oceans. It was built in France in 1918, its ship was 9 m long and two masts.

INDIAN OCEAN

Cape of Good Hope

AUSTRALIA

Sydney

Traditional boats

Since ancient times, people have built boats to navigate rivers, lakes and seas to fish or move from one place to another. Many of them are still in use today around the world as they were used centuries ago.

Construction Techniques

The traditional popular crafts used natural local materials: logs, bark or other plant elements. In some cases, the technique used was based on the casting of a log; in others, they were constructed by joining several trunks, and others, such as the reed boats of Peru and Bolivia, by twining stems of reeds, a common aquatic plant of the marshes in the region.

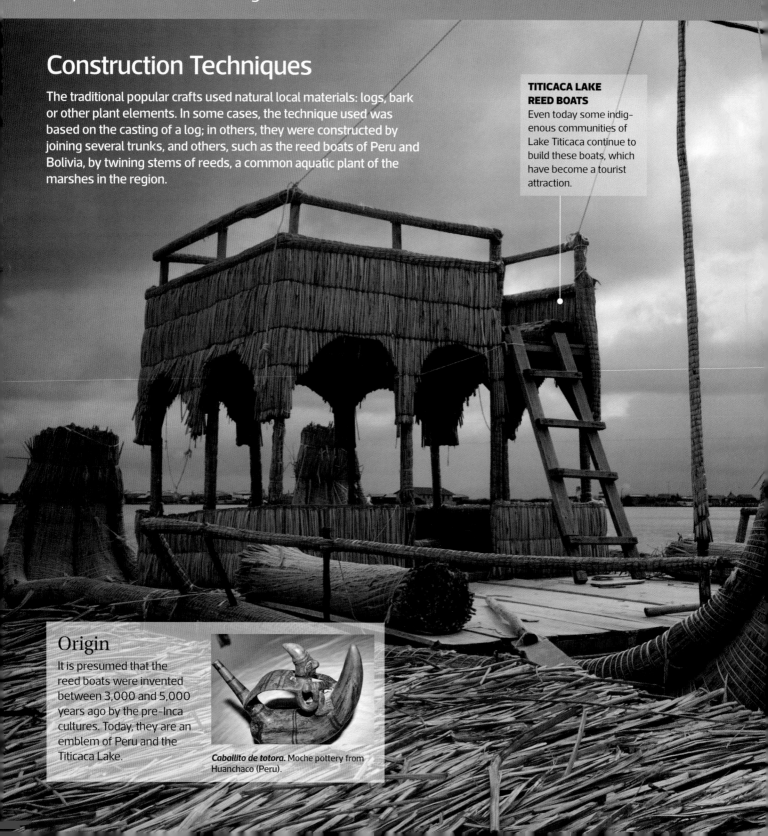

TITICACA LAKE REED BOATS
Even today some indigenous communities of Lake Titicaca continue to build these boats, which have become a tourist attraction.

Origin

It is presumed that the reed boats were invented between 3,000 and 5,000 years ago by the pre-Inca cultures. Today, they are an emblem of Peru and the Titicaca Lake.

Caballito de totora. Moche pottery from Huanchaco (Peru).

A refined technique

To build a reed raft, the collaboration of several people is necessary. Once the stalks of the plant have dried, the boat starts being shaped by tying them with pitas (rope made of plant material). The high bow and stern are achieved by straining the pitas.

CABALLITOS DE TOTORA (REED HORSES)
On the north coast of Peru, not only fishermen use these vessels. Surfing competitions are also organized with them.

FORMS
They generally have a high bow and stern. Sometimes a zoomorphic head is added, also made of reeds.

Other traditional vessels

1 Polynesian rocker canoe
It incorporates a rocker or side float to gain stability. With an ancient history, it can still be seen in Polynesia or in Indonesia.

2 Venetian gondola
Long and narrow, with one oar, gondolas were the chief means of transportation in Venice for centuries.

3 Thai Long tail
Specially designed to navigate rivers. Today, with an incorporated engine, they are still used as taxi, for distribution or touristic purposes.

4 Egyptian felucca
Sailing boat of Arab origin, it was used in ancient times in the Middle East and Northern Africa. There are still some that ply the Nile for tourist recreation.

5 Eskimo Kayak
The Eskimos were already building this kind of one-man canoe with closed cover at least 4,000 years ago to go fishing and hunting.

USS Nimitz CVN-68

Launched on May 13, 1972, this was the first nuclear aircraft carrier of a class that would be comprised by another 10 units. She is the flagship of Battle Group 11 of the US Navy; of which the Nimitz class is the backbone.

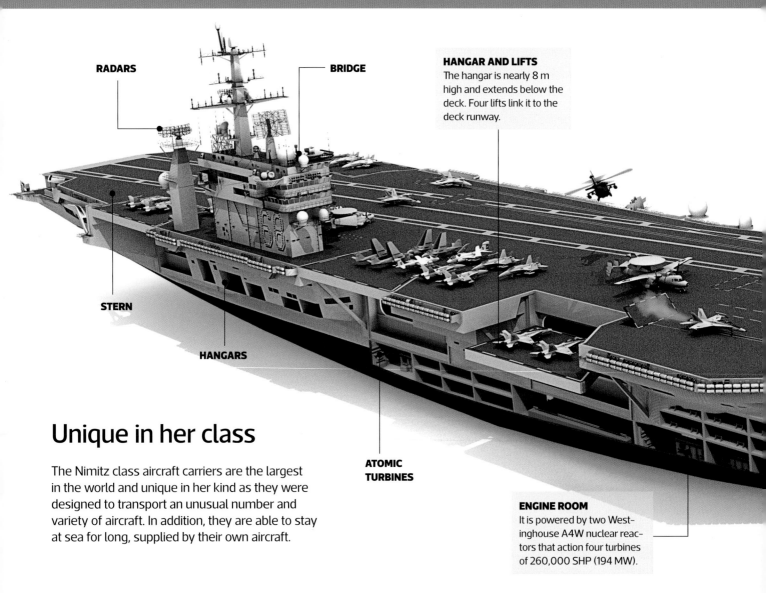

RADARS

BRIDGE

HANGAR AND LIFTS
The hangar is nearly 8 m high and extends below the deck. Four lifts link it to the deck runway.

STERN

HANGARS

ATOMIC TURBINES

ENGINE ROOM
It is powered by two Westinghouse A4W nuclear reactors that action four turbines of 260,000 SHP (194 MW).

Unique in her class

The Nimitz class aircraft carriers are the largest in the world and unique in her kind as they were designed to transport an unusual number and variety of aircraft. In addition, they are able to stay at sea for long, supplied by their own aircraft.

Aircraft she carries

She can carry 90 aircraft including 22 to 26 F-18 Hornet strike fighters, and a 6-8 "Seahawk" Helicopter Anti-submarine Squadron.

F-18 HORNET

NORTHROP GRUMMAN EA-6B PROWLER

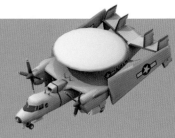

NORTHROP GRUMMAN E-2 HAWKEYE

Other large aircraft carriers

HMS HERMES
She entered into service for the British Navy in 1953 and fought in the Falklands War (1982).

USS INDEPENDENCE
She was a Forrestal-class aircraft carrier that remained in active service from 1959 to 1998.

ADMIRAL KUZNETSOV
She is the flagship of the Russian Navy and she can carry 41 aircraft.

TECHNICAL SHEET

▶ **Type:** Aircraft carrier
▶ **Crew:** 3,200 + 2,480 from air wing
▶ **Dimensions:**

332.8 m
Length

76.8 m
Beam

Provision for aircraft

Nuclear propulsion allows occupying the space for fuel with 12 million liters of gasoline and 3,000 tons of ammunition for the aircraft.

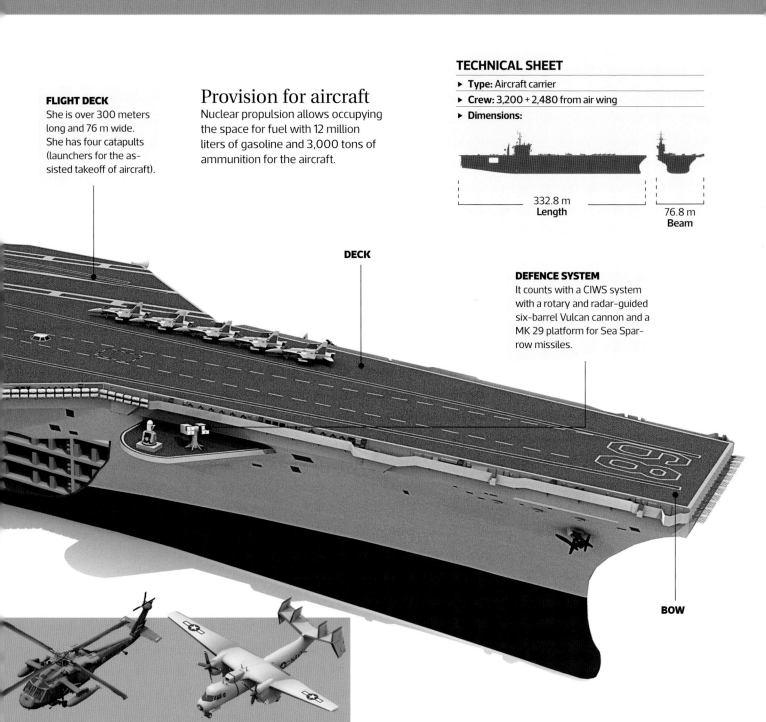

FLIGHT DECK
She is over 300 meters long and 76 m wide. She has four catapults (launchers for the assisted takeoff of aircraft).

DECK

DEFENCE SYSTEM
It counts with a CIWS system with a rotary and radar-guided six-barrel Vulcan cannon and a MK 29 platform for Sea Sparrow missiles.

BOW

SIKORSKY SH-60 SEAHAWK

GRUMMAN C-2 GREYHOUND

The *Calypso*

One of the most famous boats for scientific exploration of all time, she was originally an old Royal Navy minesweeper acquired by Jacques Cousteau for a symbolic price of 1 franc per year.

Latest technology

Cousteau equipped the Calypso with the most modern technology of her time, transforming her into an icon of ocean exploration. The Calypso had a mobile laboratory, a heliport, dive propulsion vehicles, mini submarines and underwater film cameras. With her, he began his explorations in 1951 until 1966.

THE GANTRY
It served both as a lookout point and as support for the radar antenna.

BRIDGE
The Calypso also had a very modern EDO ultrasound scanner and a radio transmitter.

NAVIGATION CONDITIONS
To improve them, the vessel was fitted with a gyro compass AOIP and a Brown autopilot.

Jacques Cousteau

Born in France, Jacques-Yves Cousteau (1910-1997) was an explorer, researcher and popularizer of oceanography. His more than 115 underwater documentaries were very popular and helped create awareness on the importance of marine conservation. He was the co-inventor of the open–circuit scuba technology used today.

IMMERSION WELL
In the center of the ship, at the height of the kitchen, an immersion well was drilled with direct access to the sea.

FAKE BOW
Underwater steel observation chamber built on the bow, 3 m underwater.

ROOMS
The crew cabins were under the deck, the one belonging to Cousteau, behind the bridge.

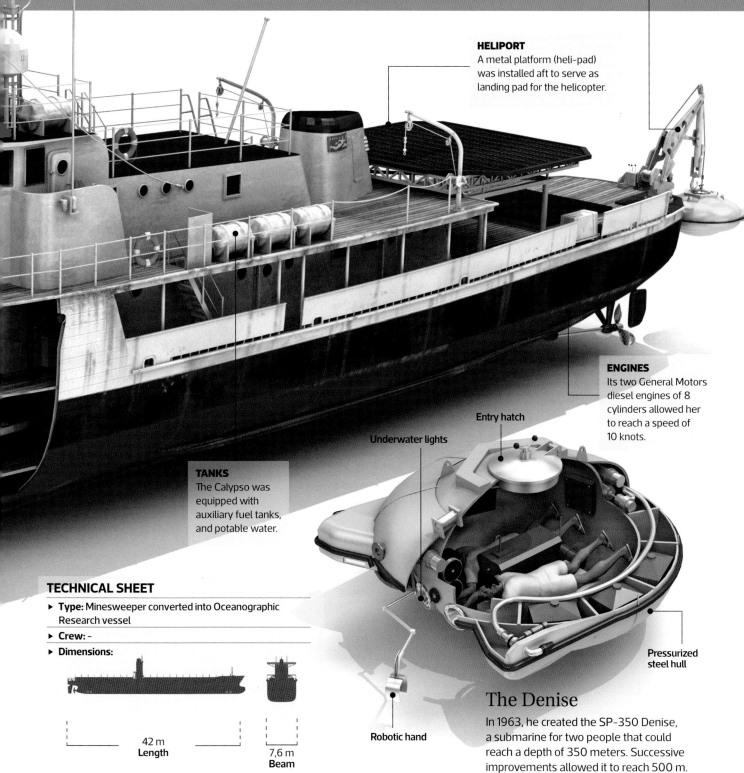

HELICOPTER
The Calypso had a light helicopter Hughes 300 which was used for various tasks, from aerial filming to crew transportation to the shore.

CRANE
The aft area was equipped with winches, cranes and a Yumbo hydraulic crane with lifting capacity for 3 tons of weight.

HELIPORT
A metal platform (heli-pad) was installed aft to serve as landing pad for the helicopter.

ENGINES
Its two General Motors diesel engines of 8 cylinders allowed her to reach a speed of 10 knots.

TANKS
The Calypso was equipped with auxiliary fuel tanks, and potable water.

Entry hatch

Underwater lights

Pressurized steel hull

Robotic hand

TECHNICAL SHEET

▶ **Type:** Minesweeper converted into Oceanographic Research vessel
▶ **Crew:** –
▶ **Dimensions:**

42 m
Length

7,6 m
Beam

The Denise

In 1963, he created the SP-350 Denise, a submarine for two people that could reach a depth of 350 meters. Successive improvements allowed it to reach 500 m.

Containerships

These giants of the sea carry all kinds of goods. Owned by Danish company A. P. Moller-Maersk, *Emma Maersk* was the world's largest container ship until 2013.

She loads everything and more

The *Emma Maersk*, launched in 2006, was the first ship built of seven of her kind. It is estimated that it could load up to 14,500 containers, though the company limits the number to a maximum of 11,000 carrying 14 tonnes. The ship can cross the Pacific in just 12 days.

LOAD
She is capable of carrying 1,400 containers more than any other ship of her kind.

HULL
Painted with silicone based paint, which prevents the leakage of biocides to the ocean.

BOW
The bulbous bow reduces fuel consumption of the ship.

DEEP
The depth of her hull, measured from deck to keel, is 30 meters.

EMMA MÆRSK

The *CMA CGM Marco Polo*

No doubt, competence of *Emma Maersk*. While she not surpassed her in size, she did in capacity. Hence she is postulated as the largest ship in the world over the *Emma Maersk*.

TECHNICAL SHEET

▸ **Type:** Containership
▸ **Crew:** Usually 13, with room for 30.
▸ **Dimensions:**

397 m
Length

56 m
Beam

TOWER
This is where the bridge and crew cabins are located.

AUXILIARY POWER
She also has five Caterpillar 8M32 generators with a total power of 40,000 hp.

MAERSK LIN

PROPELLER
Made of an alloy of copper, aluminium, nickel, iron and manganese, it weighs 131 tonnes.

Growth in size of the container ships (in tonnes)

Year	Type	Tonnes
1956	Converted Cargo Vessel	500
1970	Converted Tanker	800
1970–1980	Cellular Containership	1,000
1980	Panamax Class	3,000
1988	Panamax Class	4,000
1988–2000	Post Panamax	4,000 – 5,000
2000–2005	Post Panamax Plus	8,000
2006	Emma Maersk	15,000
2013	Maersk McKinney Moller	18,000

Engine
Wärtsilä– Sulzer 14RT-flex96C, with 109,000 horsepower. It recycles exhaust gases that are mixed with fresh air for reuse in the engine, thereby increasing efficiency by up to 12%.

Liners and cruises

The great ocean liners that lived their golden age before World War II evolved into huge and luxurious floating hotels dedicated to tourism and recreation, resulting in a new modality: the cruise.

A floating city

Launched in 2004, the *Queen Mary 2* is the world's largest ocean liner, although if considered a recreational cruise, it ranks fourth. It has 14 decks, it can carry 2620 passengers and 1253 crew members and within a wide range of options, it counts with golf courses, tennis and basketball courts, a fitness center of 2,325 m², 5 pools, a museum, a night club, casino, 14 bars, a cinema, a theater, an auditorium and even winter gardens with piano music.

TECHNICAL SHEET

▸ **Type:** Liner
▸ **Crew:** 1,253
▸ **Dimensions:**

72 m

345 m
Length

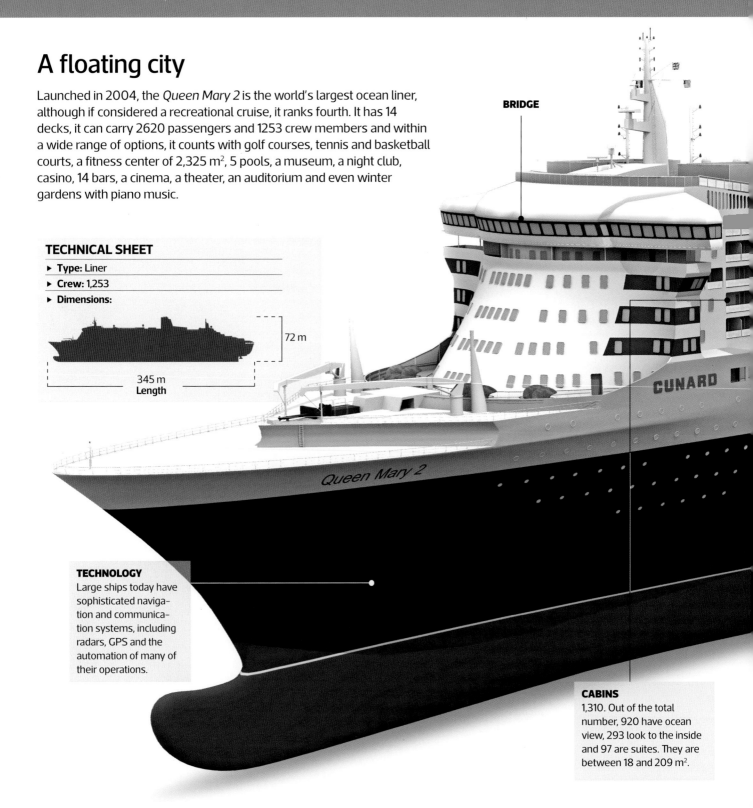

BRIDGE

CUNARD

Queen Mary 2

TECHNOLOGY
Large ships today have sophisticated navigation and communication systems, including radars, GPS and the automation of many of their operations.

CABINS
1,310. Out of the total number, 920 have ocean view, 293 look to the inside and 97 are suites. They are between 18 and 209 m².

The largest ones

361 meters long and 47 wide, the largest passenger ships in the world are two sister cruises (not liners) that belong to the shipping company Royal Caribbean International: *Oasis of the Seas* and *Allure of the Seas*. They can carry in one trip more than 6,000 passengers.

OASIS OF THE SEAS
This ship performed its maiden voyage in November 2009, while her sister was launched a year later.

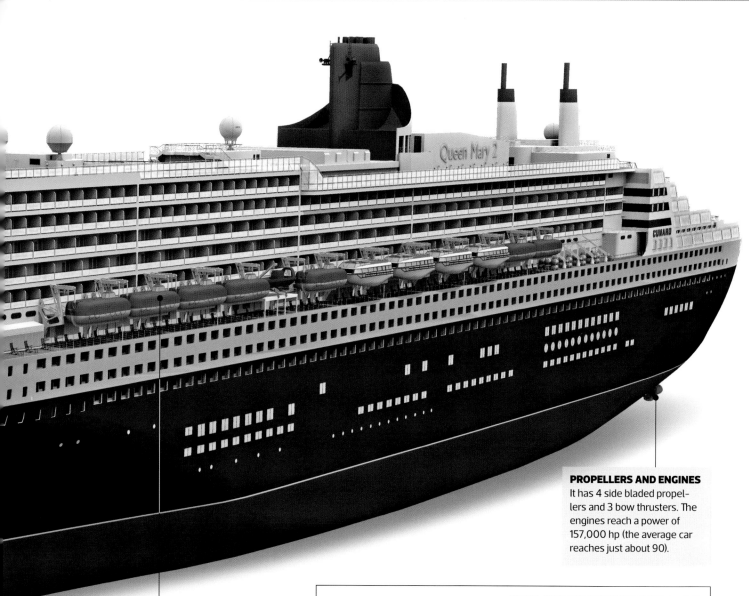

PROPELLERS AND ENGINES
It has 4 side bladed propellers and 3 bow thrusters. The engines reach a power of 157,000 hp (the average car reaches just about 90).

LIFEBOATS
They are located 25 m above the waterline to avoid damage by the waves of the North Sea.

Interior design

The design and interior decoration of *Queen Mary* refers to luxurious cruises of the past combined with contemporary décor. The artwork inside are valued at more than 3,500,000 pounds.

Luxury. Interior view of the Britannia Restaurant in *Queen Mary 2*.

Submarines

Created in the late nineteenth century, the submarine has basically stood out for its military application. Science also uses submarines for its investigations and, in recent years, it has also become possible to use them for tourism purposes.

The nuclear submarine

The submarines can run on conventional engines (petrol or diesel), but the most modern ones are nuclear powered. The first of this kind appeared in the 50s and quickly became a cornerstone for the armies of major powers. They use radioactive elements as fuel that becomes electricity in a small reactor, which gives them an almost unlimited autonomy.

HATCHES FOR MISSILE TUBES
Military submarines can launch missiles from their own tubes or from ramps and vertical silos.

MISSILE TUBES

RUDDER
To steer the submarine.

ENGINE

STERN IMMERSION RUDDER
It is operated to elevate or lower the bow.

NUCLEAR REACTOR
Works with highly enriched uranium and generates electricity that powers the engines.

How it sinks

Boats generally have positive buoyancy, i.e. its density is less than that of water, which generates a thrust towards the surface. To increase depth, a submarine needs to have a higher density than water. Therefore, it fills with air or water a series of tanks called ballasts.

Ballast tanks

To increase depth. The submarine opens the floodgates, replacing the air in ballasts with heavier water.

Ballast tanks

To emerge. Special pumps expel water from the ballasts, which is replaced by compressed air.

Underwater tourism

Slowly, submarines are being used for tourism, as well as for scientific and military purposes. There are already some examples, usually in paradise beach areas, where they plunge a few meters and allow contemplating the underwater flora and fauna through large windows.

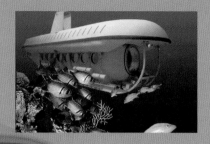

INTO THE ABYSS
Specifically modified submarines have reached depths of nearly 11,000 meters in the Mariana Trench.

SNORKEL
It is a tube used to refresh the air inside the submarine.

ANTEN

PERISCOPE
It allows seeing objects on sea surface, without emerging.

How it navigates

The submarine has no windows, not to mention that at 200 meters depth, for example, the darkness of the sea is full. To navigate, it uses a sonar, a device that works by emitting waves and then analyses how they bounce. Thus, it detects obstacles and any submerged objects.

1. The sonar emits waves

3. The sonar analyses them and determines distance.

2. When hitting an object, the wave returns to the sonar.

OW IMMERSION RUDDER

CONTROL ROOM

BATTERY

CREW CABINS

TORPEDO ROOM
Storage room for torpedoes.

SONAR ROOM AND RADIO ROOM

BALLAST
Tanks are filled with water for immersion and emptied to emerge.

Glossary

AFT Toward the rear of a ship.

ARMAMENT Military weapons and equipment.

BALLAST Any heavy material placed low in a vessel to improve its stability.

BALLISTE Catapults used in ancient warfare.

BOWSPRIT A pole extending forward from a ship's bow.

CAPSTAN A cylinder used for winding a rope or cable.

CARAVEL A small Spanish or Portuguese sailing ship of the 15th–17th centuries.

CARRACK A large European merchant ship used in the 14th to the 17th century.

CIRCUMNAVIGATION To travel all the way around the entire planet, or an island, or a continent.

FOREMAST The mast of a ship that is closest to the bow.

FORMIDABLE Inspiring fear or respect.

FUNERARY Relating to a funeral.

GALLEON A 15th–17th century sailing ship.

HEADSAIL A sail on a ship's foremast or bowsprit.

HEGEMONY Describing one country or social group's dominance over others.

KEEL The structure that runs down the bottom of a vessel's hull on which the rest of the hull is built and used to increase stability.

NAPHTHA A flammable oil containing various hydrocarbons.

PAPYRUS A material used throughout the ancient Mediterranean world for writing or painting on and also for making rope, sandals, and boats.

RUDDER A flat piece of material near the stern of a boat or ship used for steering.

SEXTANT An instrument used for measuring the angular distances between objects and especially for taking altitudes in navigation.

STARBOARD The side of a ship that is on the right when one is facing forward.

STERN The rearmost part of a ship or boat.

TRANSATLANTIC Crossing the Atlantic.

TRANSOCEANIC Crossing an ocean.

TRIREME An ancient Greek or Roman war galley with three banks of oars.

ZOOMORPHIC Representing animal forms or gods of animal form.

The Cousteau Society

Greeley Square Station

4 East 27th Street

PO Box 20321

New York, NY 10001

(212) 532-2588

Website: http://www.cousteau.org

The Cousteau Society was founded in 1973 by Captain Jacques-Yves Cousteau. Its mission is to explore the ecosystems throughout the world that have helped millions of people understand and appreciate the fragility of life on Earth

Historic Naval Ships Association

626-C Admiral Drive

Box 320

Annapolis, MD 21401

(443) 949-8341

Website: http://www.hnsa.org

The Historic Naval Ships Association (HNSA) introduces the public to historic ships from around the world.

Sail Canada

Portsmouth Olympic Harbour

53 Yonge Street

Kingston, ON, K7M 6G4

Canada

Website: http://www.sailing.ca

(613) 545-3044

Sail Canada was established in 1931 and promotes sailing in all its forms.

U.S. Naval Institute

291 Wood Road

Annapolis, MD 21402

(410) 268-6110

Website: http://www.usni.org

The U.S. Naval Institute seeks to advance the professional, literary, and scientific understanding of sea power and other issues critical to global security.

WEBSITES

Because of the changing nature of internet links, Rosen Publishing has developed an online list of websites related to the subject of this book. This site is updated regularly. Please use this link to access the list:

http://www.rosenlinks.com/VHW/ships

For Further Reading

Crawford, Steve, et al. *Battleships and Aircraft Carriers: 1900-Present.* New York, NY: Chartwell Books, 2013.

Darwin, Charles, E. J. Browne, and Michael Neve. *Voyage of the Beagle: Charles Darwin's Journal of Researches.* New York, NY: Penguin Books, 1989.

Eastland, Jonathan, and Iain Ballantyne. *HMS Victory: First Rate 1765.* Annapolis, MD: Naval Institute Press, 2011.

Grant, R. G. *Battle at Sea: 3,000 Years of Naval Warfare.* New York, NY: DK, 2008.

Johnston, Ian, and I. L. Buxton. *The Battleship Builders: Constructing And Arming British Capital Ships.* Annapolis, MD: Naval Institute Press, 2014.

Lavery, Brian. *Ship: The Epic Story of Maritime Adventure.* New York, NY: Dorling Kindersley, 2010.

Miller, William. *First Class Cargo.* Gloucestershire, England: History Press, 2016.

Philbrick, Nathaniel. *The Mayflower and the Pilgrims' New World.* New York, NY: Puffin Books, 2009.

Ross, David. *Ships: Visual Encyclopedia.* London, England: Amber Books LTD, 2010.

Ross, David. *The World's Greatest Battleships: An Illustrated History.* London, England: Amber Books LTD, 2015.

Index